THE FIRST STAGES OF MODERNIZATION IN SPANISH AMERICA

the text of this book is printed on 100% recycled paper

Crosscurrents in Latin America

Edited by Joseph S. Tulchin

Roberto Cortés Conde	THE FIRST STAGES OF MODERNIZATION IN SPANISH AMERICA
Tulio Halperin-Donghi	THE AFTERMATH OF REVOLUTION IN LATIN AMERICA
Jorge Hardoy	LATIN AMERICAN CITIES
Harmannus Hoetink	SLAVERY AND RACE RELATIONS IN THE AMERICAS
Jay Kinsbruner	CHILE: A HISTORICAL INTERPRETATION
Anthony P. Maingot	PERSONALISM IN LATIN AMERICA
Gilbert Merkx	TWENTIETH-CENTURY LATIN AMERICA
Hobart A. Spalding, Jr.	ORGANIZED LABOR IN LATIN AMERICA
Joseph S. Tulchin	LATIN AMERICA IN WORLD AFFAIRS

THE FIRST STAGES OF MODERNIZATION IN SPANISH AMERICA

ROBERTO CORTÉS CONDE

Translated from the Spanish by Toby Talbot

Harper & Row, Publishers
New York / Evanston / San Francisco / London

A hardcover edition of this book is published by Harper & Row, Publishers, Inc.

THE FIRST STAGES OF MODERNIZATION IN SPANISH AMERICA

First HARPER & ROW edition published 1974.

LIBRARY OF CONGRESS CATALOG CARD NUMBER: 73–14345

STANDARD BOOK NUMBER: 06–138419–4 (PAPERBACK)

STANDARD BOOK NUMBER: 06–136139–9 (HARDCOVER)

Designed by Ann Scrimgeour

CONTENTS

FOREWORD

The greater part of this book was written during a long winter in 1969 in Guilford, Connecticut. It is based on the courses that the author gave on the economic history of Latin America at Yale University. Different circumstances and moving from one place to another obliged the delay of its final draft, which was finished in Buenos Aires in the summer of 1971, when the author was a member of the Torcuato Di Tella Institute. Then the revision of statistical and bibliographical references delayed the final manuscript even more.

The author wishes to thank the Council of Latin American Studies and the Department of History of Yale University for the cooperation and support that he received while he was a member of the Yale faculty. He especially wishes to thank Professor Richard Morse for the opportunity of discussing with him subjects that were of common interest. Yale's excellent library was perhaps the principal factor in the preparation of this book. Later on, from afar, there were occasions when he regretted not being able to tap its resources. In Argentina the Torcuato Di Tella Institute Library was important. Whenever possible, its personnel tried to locate in other libraries the books which he needed. Mrs. Kay sustained the greatest part of the burden of these demands. Nancy López de Nisnovich contributed to the final preparation of the manuscript with her efficient collaboration, completing and revising the statistical and bibliographical references.

This study does not attempt to cover all of the Spanish American countries, nor all of their economic histories. Rather it compares five different cases of a historical experience of particular transcendence in Spanish America in the nineteenth century in five different countries—Peru, Cuba, Chile, Mexico, and Argentina. The author is aware of the long debate over the problem of the distribution of the income that was derived from international trade. Although he does not detract from its importance, he has concentrated here only on those aspects that link the export sector's growth with that of the national economy as a whole, particularly the impact and the effects of that growth.

Finally, it is pertinent to point out that the divisions into periods are, to some extent, arbitrary. In some chapters the study refers to years prior to 1850; in others, years prior to 1830. What is important, however, is that it refers to a period of unique characteristics in Spanish American history—the growth of its export economy in relation to the world's economy in the second half of the nineteenth century to World War I and, in some cases, until the crisis of 1929.

THE FIRST STAGES OF MODERNIZATION IN SPANISH AMERICA

1

THE NINETEENTH-CENTURY EXPORT ECONOMIES OF SPANISH AMERICA

By the middle of the nineteenth century the American countries which once belonged to the Spanish empire had still not recovered from the traumatic consequences of the independence movements.[1] In fact, with a few important, though isolated, exceptions, the first half of the nineteenth century was a period of economic recession resulting from a combination of causes: prolonged military conflicts, first those of the independence movement that lasted over a decade and then internal conflicts which extended into the second half of the century, the destruction of property and wealth, the assignation of a considerable portion of resources to support military operations, and the withdrawal of part of the active population from the production process.[2] Another factor contributing to the economic dislocation was the breakup of the system which had once bound the different regions of the old empire,[3] a

[1] In part this was because independence occurred amid a world counter-revolution. The prolonged resistance to acceptance of the revolutionary phenomenon in Hispanic America, which contrasted with Anglo-Saxon America, must be analyzed in relation to the different ideological climates of the two regions in different time periods. Brazil possessed its own characteristics, which are not discussed in this study because it explores only countries that formed part of the old Spanish empire.

[2] To meet the cost of military operations, the first public debt securities were issued which, in the second half of the century, weighed heavily upon the Latin American economies. Cf. J. Fred Rippy, *British Investments in Latin America 1822–1949* (Minneapolis, Minn.: University of Minnesota Press, 1959), pp. 18 et seq. Also cf. Leland H. Jenks, *The Migration of British Capital to 1875* (London: Nelson, 1963), pp. 44 et seq.

[3] Concerning early integration of intercolonial trade, see Eduardo Arcila Farías, *Comercio entre Venezuela y México* (Mexico City: El Colegio de México, 1950), chap. 1. Also see Tulio Halperin-Donghi, *Historia contemporánea de América Latina* (Madrid: Alianza Editorial, 1969), pp. 18–19; and his volume in this series *The Aftermath of Revolution* (New York, N.Y.: Harper & Row, 1973), chap. 2.

shattering of old relations and commercial circuits, and, above all, a retrogression resulting from the general isolation and wars that destroyed the dynamism in economic activity. Economic activity in Latin America generally had reached a relatively high level by the end of the eighteenth century. The old viceroyalty of Peru was one of the areas where the crisis of the colonial system was most serious. Perhaps this was due to the fact that Peru, unlike other areas of Spanish America, was suffering economic difficulties long before the Wars of Independence began. The colonial system of trade which allowed merchants from Lima to maintain control over a complex mechanism which was based upon exploitation of mineral wealth in Potosí but integrated with zones of supply in other parts of the viceroyalty, for example, the Río de la Plata with its cotton, textiles, liquor, and mules and the Capitanía General of Chile, which produced wheat, of prime importance in the Spanish diet, was dealt a mortal blow when Pacific shipping was threatened by the administrative and commercial reforms of the Spanish crown.[4] These Bourbon reforms accelerated the economic decline due, among other things, to the decline of silver production in the altiplano area.[5]

In other places, favored by special situations and relying on different economic bases, there was at the beginning of the nineteenth century a relative upswing despite the difficult circumstances of wartime. The most surprising example of this upswing probably was the Río de la Plata, more specifically, the province of Buenos Aires. Toward the end of the eighteenth century Buenos Aires shook off the limitations of its role of entrepôt where Bolivian silver was exchanged for European merchandise and found an outlet for exports of the area's natural products—leather, fats, and tallow—which began to yield unsuspected revenue. This

[4] See Guillermo Céspedes del Castillo, "Lima y Buenos Aires, repercusiones económicas y políticas de la creación del virreinato del Río de la Plata," *Anuario de estudios americanos* 8 (Seville, 1947). See also Sergio Villalobos, *El comercio y la crisis colonial* (Santiago: Ediciones de la Universidad de Chile, 1968).

[5] There is a marked difference between the situation that occurred in colonial Peru at the end of the eighteenth century and that of New Spain, which was in the process of expansion. See Alexander von Humboldt, *Ensayo político sobre el reino de la Nueva España* (Mexico City: Ed. Robledo, 1941).

trade was intensified in 1809 when, on the eve of the Revolution, Viceroy Cisneros, pressured by local interests, lifted the restriction on exporting and again after 1812 when free trade was definitively established and encouraged by a substantial price rise in cattle by-products resulting from the Napoleonic conflict.[6]

Clearly, this economic awakening, which began initially in the coastal provinces and then spread to the province of Buenos Aires, was not a general phenomenon throughout the whole territory formerly comprising the viceroyalty of Río de la Plata.[7] The earlier settled interior, the source of supply for Potosí's mining economy, had nothing to export. Worse, free trade deprived it of its littoral market, and its only alternative, Upper Peru, had been eliminated by the war. The economic problems of the interior provinces—Salta, Tucumán, and Córdoba—were aggravated further by military operations. Buenos Aires, on the other hand, enjoyed relative calm after 1820 (with the exception of the rural uprising of 1828), although it was surrounded by areas devastated by armed bands. The unsettling battles almost always occurred outside the province. Rural militias—private armies maintained by ranchers or *estancieros*—assured law and order in the province where a steady cattle stock provided products that could be exported.

Buenos Aires could participate in the international market under extremely favorable conditions because of the low cost of cattle exploitation: first, it was near the Atlantic, and second, extensive cattle raising requires virtually no labor supply or, at most, only labor of a seasonal and hence migratory nature.[8] The society to which this production structure corresponded—one of sparse and scattered population—permitted the landowners to impose order on the countryside, thereby insuring a stable regime and a firm

[6] See the graph on meat prices in W. Stanley Jevons, "On the Variation of Prices and the Value of the Currency Since 1872," in E. M. Carus Wilson, *Essays in Economic History* (London: Edward Arnold, Publisher, Ltd. 1966), p. 26.

[7] Tulio Halperin-Donghi, "La Expansión ganadera en la campaña bonaerense (1810–1852)," *Desarrollo Económico* 3 (April–September 1963): 57.

[8] Azara's example of ten people for a ranch of 10,000 hectares (1 hectare =2.47 acres) is frequently cited in the literature dealing with this topic. During branding periods, when animals were marked and a roundup was necessary, more personnel was required.

social order, all at a low cost. These elements taken together made possible the opening up of the Argentine economy to foreign trade in the first half of the nineteenth century. This not only implies the presence of certain economic assumptions, namely, the Río de la Plata's comparative advantage in extensive cattle production, but also political and social requisites which were absent in other areas of Spanish America.

The hide trade, however, did not signify the initiation of the complex mechanism which would subsequently integrate the Argentine economy with the world market. Cattle exploitation only assumed the opening of export possibilities based on a specialization in accord with available resources. With its limited capital and labor supply but with abundant land, the Río de la Plata turned to extensive cattle production. This same situation, which explains the failure of agriculture at that time (scarcity of population on the one hand and lack of transportation on the other), was the result of the fact that production adapted itself to existing resources.[9] In order to promote the export of hides, there was no need—as there would be later on—for large-scale importation of capital and labor which the country lacked. To the extent that the early orientation of its exports did not require modification in the proportions of its resources but, rather, utilization of existing ones, this is almost a unique case in America.

In contrast, most of the export activities of Spanish America, as they achieved increasing importance in the nineteenth century, demanded the incorporation in varying proportions of certain production factors which did not exist previously such as capital, labor, and so forth. Thus, in these cases the development of export activity was not simply the result of a more efficient allocation of existing resources between the domestic sector and exports; it required the incorporation from other areas of the factors of production that were lacking.[10] This was true in the cases of guano in

[9] This contradicts Burgin's belief regarding the failure of colonizing attempts as a consequence of the opposition of cattle raisers. See Miron Burgin, *The Economic Aspects of Argentine Federalism* (Cambridge, Mass.: Harvard University Press, 1946).

[10] See Jonathan V. Levin, *The Export Economies* (Cambridge, Mass.: Harvard University Press, 1960). See also Robert Baldwin, *Economic Development and Export Growth* (Berkeley and Los Angeles, Calif.: University of California Press, 1964), chap. 1.

Peru (1840 to 1880), the sugar industry in Cuba, mining in Chile, as well as agriculture in the Pampas after 1870, which differed substantially from the early export activity in the Río de la Plata.

Guano, bird excrement deposited for years upon the Chinchas and Lobos islands in Peru, had existed ever since Incan times. Its large-scale exploitation, however, was impracticable without relying on substantial contributions of capital and labor, which were both lacking in Peru in the year 1840.[11] Once capital was obtained and labor imported, export of guano paved the way for a period of economic expansion based on foreign trade.

The expansion of the economy based on its exporting sector was thus not only a consequence of exploitation of an abundant resource, but was made possible, primarily and fundamentally, at least in the historical experience of the Latin American countries, through the incorporation of resources that were scarce in these areas, which had to be combined in some way with existing ones in order to allow the production of these resources to enter the market. In each case the mobile factors of production, labor and capital, varied in accordance with the relative supply and the nature of the resources to be exploited. The question was not, however, simply one of reallocation of resources between domestic and foreign production. It was a question of selling a surplus resource.[12] That output was directed toward foreign markets,

[11] See chapter 2.

[12] This is what Myint's thesis points out. Hence, it should be analyzed here according to the *vent for surplus* theory. See H. Myint, "The Classical Theory of International Trade and the Underdeveloped Countries," *The Economic Journal* 68 (1958): 321. There he says:

> The comparative-costs theory assumes that the resources of a country are given and fully employed before it enters into international trade. The function for trade is then to reallocate its given resources more efficiently between domestic and export production in the light of the new set of relative prices now open to the country. With given techniques and full employment, export production can be increased only at the cost of reducing the domestic production. In contrast, in the "vent for surplus" theory, trade possesses a surplus productive capacity of some sort or another. The function of trade here is not so much to reallocate the given resources as to provide the new effective demand for the output of the surplus resources which would have remained unused in the absence of trade. It follows that export production can be increased without necessarily reducing domestic production.

and therefore, stemmed not from the fact that some production factors came from abroad, but, more importantly, from the lack of markets for these products in the countries where they were exploited. In some instances this lack of markets was due to a scarcity of people, but in most cases, it was due to their extremely low incomes.

Though there were common features in the forms which this phenomenon assumed in Spanish America, the responses and adjustment to these circumstances were not generally the same. They depended mostly on the nature of the particular structure of each area where this experience was observed, although there were characteristics common to the different areas under consideration, such as flows of capital or labor to develop a resource for a foreign market. The variety of responses depended not only on physical differences, geological and ecological, but also on political and, more generally, on cultural differences. The specific features of each case thus corresponded to the geophysical characteristics and the resources of each region, as well as to its particular heritage which stemmed from its own history and conditioned its subsequent development.[13]

[13] The technological nature (production functions) would be determined to a great extent (according to Baldwin) by the nature of the resources in the region or by the initial conditions under which the exploitation of these natural resources is produced. Baldwin distinguishes two agricultural models which produce different effects on the development of the region, the family-sized farm and the plantation. Robert E. Baldwin, "Patterns of Development in Newly Settled Regions," in John Friedman and William Alonso, eds., *Regional Development and Planning* (Cambridge, Mass.: The M.I.T. Press, 1964).

For similar cases in the economic history of the United States, North has tried to answer the question of why some regions have not been able to depart from a single-product export structure while others have attained important levels of urbanization and industrialization. North maintains it lies in the following: (a) the region's resources at a given technological level, (b) the character, that is, the technological nature, of the export industry, and (c) the technological changes and transference costs. He adds that the natural conditions of the region determine what commodities will be exported. The character—the technological nature—of the exportable production (the production function) has important consequences and influences its future development. North also differentiates two types of agricultural production: the plantation and the family-sized farm. The first one is relatively labor-intensive and has significant economies of scale. Besides, it is reflected

Cuba has always possessed natural conditions propitious to the cultivation of sugar. The delay in its development, however, for several centuries after the development of sugar cultivation in Brazil, for example, was due to the restrictions on free trade and importation of labor during the Spanish colonial period and to the existence of a society of small- and medium-sized landholders which was less conducive to a plantation economy. The greater mobilization of labor provided an important incentive for the investment of capital in the sugar industry, but it was only by a technological and structural modification in production that it received strong impetus. A sustained flow of capital funds, both a prerequisite and a consequence, was further assured by juridical and political guarantees which, from the point of view of the country that was the object of these guarantees, was tantamount to the abnegation of the country's right to self-government.

Copper exploitation in Chile, which toward the end of the nineteenth century was declining because of increasing costs and lower prices, not only required greater available capital funds, but also the presence of technology to which the domestic sector did not have access. Corporations or individuals with experience in other parts of the world were able to incorporate techniques acquired elsewhere and the machinery that was needed to apply them to the productive processes that was not yet accessible to those with only capital at their disposal. It cannot be said that Chilean society at the beginning of the twentieth century was completely lacking in capital funds. At the same time that North American companies were investing in copper, Chilean capitalists were purchasing lands in Argentina. This indicates a rather common occurrence in Latin America at that time. Availability of capital is not sufficient. It is necessary also to have potential access to other factors by a particular sector of production, which means knowledge and the absence of certain monopolies on knowledge, whether these be in technology or in channels of distribution. The quasi monopoly of technology in addition to a high volume of capital gradually placed

in an unequal distribution of income and different attitudes toward investment and growth. See Douglas North, "Agriculture in Regional Economic Growth," *Journal of Farm Economics,* vol. 41, no. 5 (December 1959), pp. 945–946. On the Chilean case see Jay Kinsbruner, *Chile: A Historical Interpretation* (New York: Harper & Row, 1973), chap. 6.

the major portion of Chilean copper export in the hands of three foreign companies.

The situation differed in the Río de la Plata where the coastal economy had been oriented toward exports since the eighteenth century. The nature of its resources determined an extensive type of production: cattle raising to produce hides emphasized the preexisting demographic vacuum of the Pampas. Lack of both labor and means of transportation to ports during the first part of the nineteenth century hampered the development of agriculture, whereas in a country less richly endowed with land, such as Chile, agriculture was more advantageous because labor and transportation were available. After 1870 foreign capital investments, encouraged by government action, established the infrastructural basis of transportation, which, along with the entry of a large mass of people needed to work in these areas, made agriculture and, in turn, the production of cattle for meat viable in the formerly deserted Pampas. Thus, while production for the export sector was in the hands of residents, the same was not true of marketing, manufacture, and transportation, all of which were in the hands of foreign firms. Perhaps what largely distinguishes the case of the Río de la Plata are the consequences for social stratification and distribution of income (and consequently the economic effects which that activity produced) which resulted from the impact of a large mass of people that went to work in agriculture and lived in a market economy where consumer expectations existed from the beginning.[14]

[14] Regarding the family-sized farm agriculture and its effects on income distribution cf. North, "Agriculture in Regional Economic Growth," pp. 945–946. Referring to its effects on the development North says (pp. 949–950):

> A positive restatement of the thesis elaborated above is that the development of a successful agricultural export industry will result in an increase in income to the region, and under the favorable conditions outlined above will lead to:
>
> 1. Specialization and division of labor with a widening of the regional market;
> 2. The growth of facilities and subsidiary industry to efficiently produce and market the export commodity;
> 3. The development of residentiary industry to serve local consumers, some of which may, in consequence of expanding markets and external econ-

In Mexico the Científicos' yearnings for modernization broke up to a great extent a preexisting order. Nevertheless, Mexico's entire development during and after the regime of Porfirio Díaz bears the mark of a society whose basic characteristics were already drawn in the eighteenth century following the adjustments to its initial contact with Europe, the demographic catastrophe of the seventeenth century, and the impact of colonization.[15]

In the following pages we shall attempt not only to isolate the common features of this process within nineteenth-century Spanish American economies (at least in the cases studied), but also to note the extent of their differences and the circumstances and factors which provoked their dissimilar responses.

This export boom, or this growth through exports, was translated in general into significant changes in societies that were emerging from long decades of wars, isolation, and backwardness to begin a first stage toward modernization in their economies, societies, and polities, with the consequent variations and complications that are described in the following chapters.

---

omies developed in association with the export industry, lead to a broadening in the export base;

4. As a natural consequence of the above conditions, the growth of urban areas and facilities;
5. An expanded investment in education and research to broaden the region's potential.

Under these circumstances, a good deal of industrial development will occur naturally as a consequence of the conditions described above. Indeed as the regional market increases in size, more and more manufacturing firms will find it feasible to establish branch plants there.

[15] This aspect is developed in chapter 5. See Woodrow Borah, "New Spain's Century of Depression," *Iberoamericana* 35 (June 1951).

2

PERU IN THE AGE OF GUANO

During the entire eighteenth century Peru experienced the consequences of a prolonged crisis, the result of structural problems and of persistent unfavorable contingencies. Changes in the structure of colonial world trade, replacement of the fleet system and of the monopoly in the distribution of European goods that accompanied permission to sail around Cape Horn, the loss of the Upper Peruvian and even the Chilean markets due to the rise of a new area oriented to the Atlantic, all produced this crisis in the once-prosperous Peruvian economy. In addition to the commercial crisis affecting a complex system of economic relations whose resources had their origin in the silver of Potosí, Chilean agriculture, and northern Argentina's cotton and textile output and whose facilities for distribution, commercialization, credit, and capital were in Lima, the dominant center,[1] there was simultaneously a steady slump in silver output as well as in mercury from Huancavelica, which was used to form amalgams. This was in sharp contrast to New Spain's prosperity in the eighteenth century.[2]

A substitute for the earnings derived from selling minerals on the world market could not be found here, as it could in other monocultural zones, in reliance on the earnings of agricultural products—sugar and cotton—which had existed in Peru since early times. Alongside the agricultural producers, whose output figured to a greater or lesser degree in the market economy, there existed a very extensive subsistence sector of the population in a

[1] A complete description of the complex structure of Peruvian economic relations may be found in Guillermo Céspedes del Castillo, "Lima y Buenos Aires, repercusiones económicas y políticas de la creación del virreinato del Río de la Plata," *Anuario de estudios americanos* 8 (Seville, 1947).

[2] In reference to this, see Baron Alejandro de Humboldt, *Ensayo político sobre Nueva España,* 2 vols. (Paris: Lecointe, 1836).

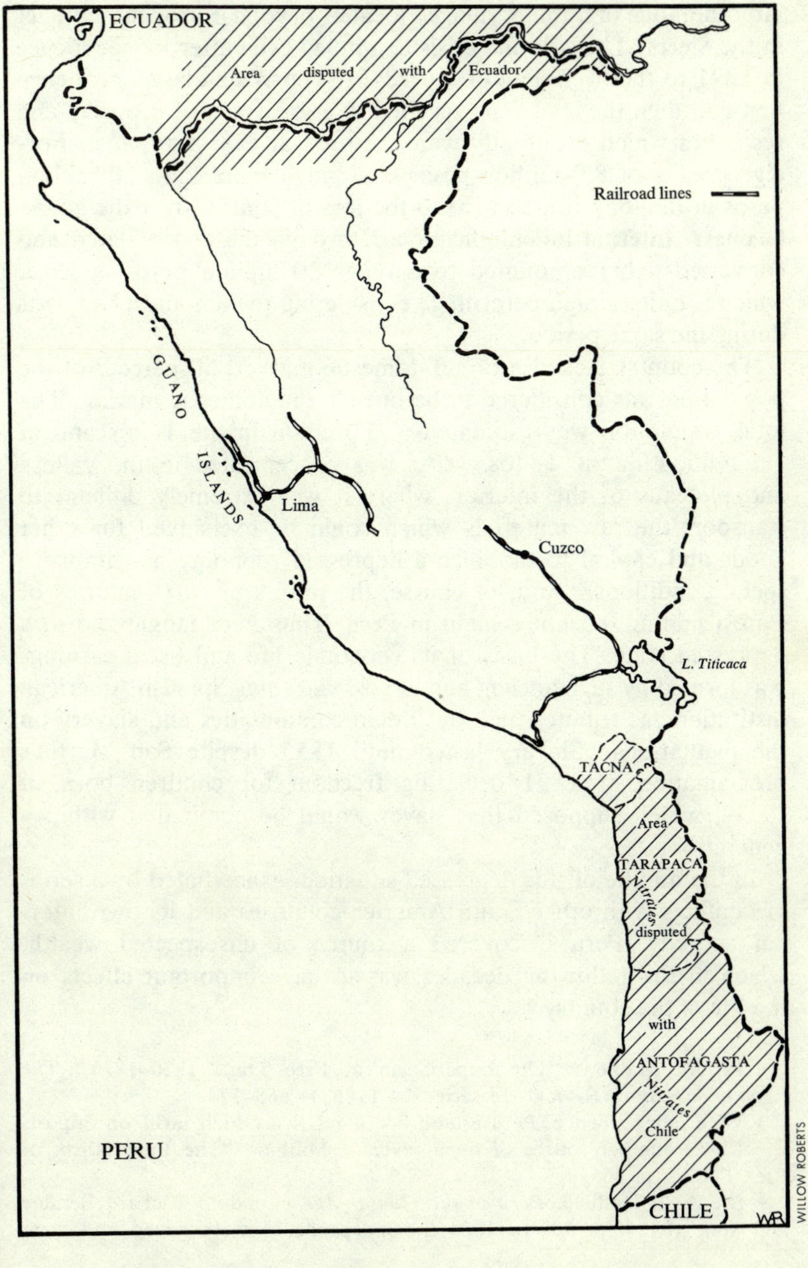

ECUADOR
Area disputed with Ecuador
Railroad lines
GUANO ISLANDS
Lima
Cuzco
L. Titicaca
TACNA
Area
TARAPACA
Nitrates
disputed
with
ANTOFAGASTA
Nitrates
Chile
PERU
CHILE
WR
WILLOW ROBERTS

large number of Indian villages located beyond European contact in the Sierra. The colonial crisis continued even after independence in 1821 to the beginning of the 1840s. The Wars of Independence first and then the civil wars resulted in a great loss of property and resources which eventually were restored at exorbitant cost. Foreign credits of 8.9 million pesos cost much more than 20 million pesos in the long run and led to the loss of control over the guano business. Internal indemnifications (through the consolidated and converted debt) amounted to another 20 million pesos at least, which is quite a high percentage considering the amount of exports during the same period.

The country lacked a broad domestic market; 80 percent of the population was considered to be outside the domestic market. The total population was estimated at 1 million in the 1820s and at 1.5 million in the 1840s. Most was concentrated in the valleys and plateaus of the interior, where it was extremely difficult to transport the raw materials which could be exchanged for other goods and capital to mobilize a depressed economy and improve social conditions.[3] And, of course, the profits of two centuries of Potosí mining did not remain in Peru. Thus Peru languished in a depressed state. The basis of its economic life and fiscal earnings was formed by such ancient and almost vanishing Spanish American institutions as tributes paid by Indian communities and slavery on the plantations.[4] Slavery lasted until 1855 despite San Martín's proclamation of 1821 declaring freedom for children born of slaves, which supposed that slaves would be eliminated within a generation.

In the middle of this depressed situation, exacerbated by a series of conflicts with other South America countries and its own internal anarchy, Peru discovered a source of unsuspected wealth, which in the following decades was to have important effects on the life of the country.[5]

[3] W. M. Mathew, "The Imperialism of Free Trade 1820–1870," *The Economic History Review*, 2d series, 21 (1968): 568–574.

[4] With independence, Peru established a relatively high tariff on imports which was another source of fiscal revenue. Mathew, "The Imperialism of Free Trade," p. 565.

[5] See A. J. Duffield, *Peru in the Guano Age* (London: Richard Bentley and Son, 1877), p. 73. In 1824 the independence wars ended and were

The cold coastal currents off Peru make its climate belie its tropical location. They also account for the dryness of the coastal zone, which requires irrigation for cultivation. These factors, which constituted an agricultural disadvantage in the central zone, accounted for the accumulation of enormous deposits of animal excrement in the islands off the coast of Peru. The coldness of the water (the Humboldt current) attracted fish and, hence, birds. The atmospheric dryness permitted the preservation and calcination of their deposits, which had a high concentration of nitrogen.

Though unknown as fertilizer in the rest of the world, guano, which takes its name from the Indian word for the *guanay* bird, had been utilized as such in Incan times to improve the yield of crops on unproductive lands. Though abandoned during the colonial period when mining was the focal point of economic activity, its use as a fertilizer was emphasized by Manuel E. Rivero and by Liebig in 1841. In 1830 the government authorized duty-free extraction of guano in order to provide aid to declining agriculture. And in 1840 guano extraction for export purposes began to be considered. The first shipment of guano sent to Great Britain arrived in Liverpool in 1841, and a price of about 18 pounds per ton was paid for it.[6] A Peruvian entrepreneur, Francisco de Quiroz, the president of the Chamber of Commerce, proposed paying the government 10,000 pesos per year in exchange for the exclusive concession rights to extract guano for a period of six years. He advanced 40,000 of the total 60,000 pesos into the fiscal coffers. However, only 1,500 of this advance was in cash, the remaining 38,500 was in government certificates.

The government, in need of funds, imposed the forced sale of government securities on a reluctant public and then accepted those securities at par in payment of fiscal obligations. These securities were negotiable on the open market at a considerable discount from their nominal value, and Quiroz took advantage of these circumstances to pay a considerably lower amount.

When it was learned through a letter from the British agents that guano was expected to sell at 12 pounds per ton, which Quiroz

---

followed by civil strife among the Peruvians themselves, followed by conflicts with Colombia, Bolivia, Chile, and Argentina.

6 Mathew, "The Imperialism of Free Trade," p. 568.

and his partner Aquiles Allier maintained they had not foreseen, a flurry of protest ensued over the unfavorable conditions that the government had accepted in the contract with Quiroz. Meanwhile Quiroz and Allier approached the government and offered it a larger share in the profits.[7]

We quote extensively from the central document of the first guano negotiation because it is most expressive of the characteristics of those contracts which later gave place to never-ending lawsuits and conflicts. This is what the people involved report about the controversial alternatives:

> As soon as it became known in Lima through the Liverpool correspondence which arrived on the English vessel, *Dyron,* that guano had been sold for as much as one hundred twenty pesos per ton [a real craze took hold of everyone], we were attacked with the greatest vehemence, and Sr. Colmenares who was serving as Attorney General of the Supreme Court went so far as to request an embargo on Francisco Quiroz's property for having employed fraud and deceit in tricking the government into the contract that had been signed.
>
> Meanwhile, the Hon. Sr. Menendez had ordered Francisco Quiroz to be summoned in order to agree upon a change in the leasing contract, whereupon a new contract was indeed drawn up with the President and Sr. Cano, Minister of the Treasury, whereby the leasing concession continued to operate but with the stipulation that the government would receive two-thirds of the liquid output [profit] from guano, and the remaining share would belong to the lessees. The rough draft of this new contract was drawn up, and was dispatched to be put into final form for signing and publication. At that point, the Hon. Sr. Menendez informed Francisco Quiroz that since the matter was arranged and concluded, and the government was entering into a partnership in the venture, it seemed only natural and proper for the government to know as much about the venture as we did and that he hoped we would have no objection to showing him the correspondence [on the subject] that had been received from Europe.
>
> Though the new contract had not yet been signed, in view of the Hon. Sr. Menendez's request for our correspondence and operating under the assumption that the matter was arranged and concluded according to mutually agreed terms, we felt it would be an insult to

[7] *Exposición que Don Francisco Quirós y Don Aquiles Allier Elevaron Al Soberano Congreso* (Lima: Imprenta del Correo Peruano, 1845). Reprinted in Joseph S. Tulchin, ed., *Problems in Latin American History* (New York: Harper & Row, 1973), pp. 165–172.

the President of the Republic to doubt his good faith and suspect him capable of going back on his word; and thus as gentlemen, we granted him access to our correspondence.

Whereupon the Hon. Sr. Menendez and his Ministers saw the confirmation slip sent us by Mr. Wm. Jos. Meyers and Co. on the sale of seven thousand tons of guano for which they awaited delivery, two thousand of which was priced at eighteen sterling pounds (or ninety pesos) and the remaining five thousand at a floating conditional price, subject to the item's retail price.

Reading the sale notification undoubtedly produced an extraordinary sensation in the Hon. Sr. Menendez's mind, for instead of signing the document agreed upon the previous night whereby, in his own words, the matter was arranged and concluded, he summoned us two days after having extracted our correspondence with these same words, and in the palace in the presence of his Ministers informed us that it was being publicly rumored that he had been bought off by us through a gift of five hundred thousand pesos, and that since such rumors were injurious to his reputation, he had resolved not to participate in this venture but to turn it over to the Supreme Court, which would render a verdict on the question, and having said this, he ordered our correspondence to be returned to us.

The Cabinet [Excmo. Consejo de Estado] was overcome by the same vertigo that was affecting everyone, several of its members proposed authorizing the Executive Power to dispose immediately of one or two million pesos of guano, which made the annulment of our leasing contract indispensable. To this end, an agreement was reached, thus paving the way for conceivably an act that was probably unique in the class.

Our anticipations, from what had been said as well as what had been written, were fulfilled; everyone clamored for the annulment of our contract; prior to its annulment, all came forth with the most advantageous proposals for the public treasury; but when the moment itself arrived, everyone backed out. The government, seeing that no one came forth with an acceptable offer, having summoned the bidders through the official press, was again disillusioned, and admitted that its conduct with us had been unfair and imprudent. The Hon. Sr. Menendez sent for Francisco Quiroz, and Sr. General La Fuente contacted Aquiles Allier for us to reenter negotiations with the government and to assume the guano business again under the same conditions that we had agreed upon previously. At first, we resisted since it seemed that after what had happened, we would be exposed to further unpleasantness and annoyances, but finally we acceded, and the Hon. Sr. Menendez, after having received our verbal acceptance from Francisco Quiroz, seized the latter's hands, pressed them in his own, and assured him that he would never forget

> the service we were rendering to the government and to him in particular by relieving him of this affair that weighed so heavily upon him.
>
> In view of our acceptance, we met that same night at the home of Dr. Cano, Minister of the Treasury. There we agreed upon the terms of the contract, wherein it was stipulated that we would waive thirty of the forty thousand pesos which we had advanced as payment for the first four-year lease of guano deposits, of which only one had elapsed, and we would advance two hundred eighty-seven thousand pesos on account for the shares belonging to the government in the transaction, in exchange for which we were to be granted a five-year concession to export guano abroad. As a result of this agreement, we paid the first installment of eighty-seven thousand pesos, receiving the Minister's assurance that he had signed it Su Excelencia [the President] and that the decree would appear in the next issue of the "Peruano."
>
> Imagine our surprise when we saw that instead of publishing the arrangement that had been agreed and stipulated between us, what appeared contained important variations, of which we had not been informed at all, substituting five years for one obligatory year and four voluntary years, and the word Europe for abroad.[8]

Nevertheless, all did not end there. The Peruvian government subsequently resolved to limit the agreement to one year and after the four-year voluntary period which expired on February 19, 1842, to accept bids from other firms besides Quiroz and Allier. While these events were underway, arousing much interest and undisguised greed in Lima, in England the market had lost its early optimism.

MacDonald and Company, the principal intermediary and a powerful purchaser, admitted that in the months when demand should have been highest, even their name could not inspire confidence in farmers. Using the new Peruvian contract as a pretext, it rescinded its purchasing commitments with Meyers and Company and refused to receive the merchandise precisely when Quiroz and Allier were pressed to meet government payments and had issued letters of credit against Meyers for the shipments which Meyers could no longer sell, at least not under the original stipulations. Using the same argument—the new contract—Meyers protested the letters of credit, thereby unleashing the first of many waves of

[8] Ibid., pp. 167–169.

protest and claims which this tumultuous transaction was eventually to undergo.[9]

It was undoubtedly difficult, especially under the conditions existing in the 1840s or prior to that period, for that matter, to find within Peru sufficient capital to support an enterprise which, despite showing promise of high returns, required a tremendous investment to get underway. This explains the increasingly active role assumed by British firms.

It is necessary at this juncture to clarify an aspect which will be discussed later on. Guano itself (independently of payments to the state) required a significant capital investment in ships, warehouses, transportation, lodging, and wages. Around 1840, due to the aforementioned circumstances—scarce or nonexistent domestic capital during the colonial mining period, a prolonged crisis, devastation, and so forth—nonfixed capital was extremely scarce and could not be mobilized for investment. Further testimony to this fact comes from discussions later in the century of the problem of consolidation of the national debt as a measure for incorporating capital into a depressed domestic market. The beginning of the exploitation of guano in these circumstances seemed to require the utilization of foreign capital.

Because Quiroz had extraordinary obligations requiring immediate cash, he resorted not to his fellow-countrymen in the Chamber of Commerce but to his British partners who, through their connections, obtained additional funds that, in the end, converted them into the most important partners. Guano prices dropped with the discovery of deposits on the British islands of Ichabone in the South Pacific, which provided a new source of supply for the British market. In the year 1845 guano imports to Great Britain from Africa amounted to 254,527 tons; in 1846 imports from Peru only came to 25,100 tons. Africa's advantage derived from its low price of five to eight pounds per ton, against the cost of ten pounds for Peruvian guano.[10] Nevertheless, by

9 Banco Italiano, Lima, *El Perú en marcha, Ensayo de geografía económica* (Lima, 1941), p. 100.

10 Although in the twentieth century there was some recovery, guano never regained the same importance as an export activity as it enjoyed during the golden age following 1840.

TABLE 2–1 BRITISH IMPORTS OF PERUVIAN GUANO
(*in thousands of tons*)

1845	14.1	1848	64.2
1846	25.1	1849	73.6
1847	59.4	1850	95.1

SOURCE: Mathew, "The Imperialism of Free Trade," p. 570.

1847 the deposits of Ichabone were exhausted, and a new period of expansion began for Peru.

During the period of depressed prices, the government continued demanding advances from the lessees. This meant that only those with strong reserves could meet the requirements of the undertaking. These continued demands for advances were the result of an unsound fiscal policy based on the government's insistence on a direct share of guano rather than a tax on the income produced by the exploitation of that resource. And, further, in a relatively unprosperous society struggling to preserve its dwindling wealth, guano replaced exports which had been an important source of government revenue.

THE PROBLEM OF THE PUBLIC DEBT AND THE MECHANISM OF CONSIGNMENTS

The foreign debt was to become one of the problems affecting the mechanism of marketing guano and distributing the profits derived from its sale. The second decade of the nineteenth century witnessed an original experiment in mobilizing capital from the Old World to the New. An increasing number of small English holders of savings, encouraged by the optimistic description of their fellow-countrymen, invested funds in the newly established republics of the former Spanish empire.[11] This action resulted in

[11] See Leland H. Jenks, *Our Cuban Colony* (New York: The Vanguard Press, 1928). Also see J. Fred Rippy, *British Investments in Latin America 1822–49* (Minneapolis, Minn.: University of Minnesota Press, 1959), p. 18.

part from the sympathy felt by potential investors in England for the Hispanic American revolutions and in part from the depressed price trend on the European continent following the Napoleonic Wars. The Spanish American countries, deprived of resources due to the loss of mineral sources (Potosí, for example, belonged alternately to Río de la Plata and Peru) or faced with declines in production because of the impossibility of collecting revenues in a period marked by war, yet with heavy obligations to sustain armies and military operations, did not hesitate in the face of an obviously dubious political future to commit their future earnings to assure government subsistence and to reach political stability.

Peru was no exception. In 1822 it negotiated a loan in London for 1.8 million pounds. The hazards of the Wars of Independence and regional struggles did not help to stabilize Peruvian finances. In 1825 the country quickly recognized its inability to pay not only the capital on the British loan, but also the interest which in the ensuing years accumulated in alarming proportions. The capital debt, which in 1825 had risen to 8.9 million *soles,* had by 1840 accumulated interest for another 8 million, which, added to the original capital, amounted to a multiplication of the interest to the point where over 500,000 soles annually were required just to service the debt.

As long as Peru was known only for its wars and revolutions, holders of securities, which were being quoted at 16 percent of their nominal value, had no recourse other than to suffer default. Nevertheless, news of the new guano bonanza brought increasing pressure upon both British and Peruvian authorities to obtain some payment on the bonds. Despite much hesitation and official pressure from the United Kingdom, which, however, never reached the point of direct action, the stockholders' efforts, after various alternatives, proved successful and thus determined that definitive control of the guano trade would be held by the British.[12]

This leads to an explanation of the mechanism by which guano products were marketed. The most common procedure at the time, in risky international transactions or where adequate information concerning the market was lacking, was that of consignment. Producers consigned merchandise to merchant shippers who as-

12 On this subject, see Mathew, "The Imperialism of Free Trade."

sumed responsibility for its sale and collected freightage and storage costs plus a commission on the sale. For guano the commission had been established as a percentage on sales volume which led immediately to serious dissension between the Peruvian government and the lessees and to equally notorious maneuvers to subordinate the sale price to volume, which favored the lessees. While the government, which in practice enjoyed almost a total monopoly of supply, tried to impose high prices, the consignees, interested in the volume of the transaction, sought to increase sales. Since in reality the latter were effectively in charge of sales in a market extremely distant from the consignor, the lessees in general leaned toward low prices and sought greater sales volume. One can assume that in order to increase their profits at times they presented declarations of costs that were considerably inflated, which is quite conceivable in view of the Peruvian government's lack of control over sales. As regards the claims of the holders of Peruvian bonds, the first agreement which was reached in 1849 at the same time that a contract was granted to the firm of Anthony Gibbs provided that the consignee (Gibbs) could redeem the debt securities from bondholders at their current market value, which was then quoted at 40 percent less than its nominal or par value. Gibbs, in turn, was authorized to pay 50 percent of what it owed the government from the sale of guano in these same bonds, but at their face value. In other words, the government accepted the bonds at par when it could have purchased them on the open market for 40 percent less. Many people gained by speculating with this business.

In order to insure that these funds fell into the hands of British holders of Peruvian securities and to avoid defrauding British investors, a British company was to supervise receipts from the sale of guano in the United Kingdom. In this manner, all of the trade remained in British hands despite the most emphatic declarations, beginning with the Congressional Resolution of 1849, concerning the obligation to provide preference for nationals.[13]

[13] On November 6, 1849, Congress resolved that Peruvian citizens would receive preference in contracts for guano concessions. See Jorge Basadre, *Historia de la República del Perú,* vol. I (Lima: Editorial Cultura Antártica S.A., 1946), p. 229. See also Jonathan V. Levin, *The Export Economies* (Cambridge, Mass.: Harvard University Press, 1960).

By the end of the 1850s the consignment system aroused enormous criticism. The conflict between the government and the consignees and a general lack of confidence were aggravated by low prices. Although Castilla in his second presidential term tried to enforce the Resolution of 1849, the Peruvians were not in a position to assume responsibility for the operation, and the only change for the moment was the diversification of concessions through the extension of contracts to various European firms.[14]

One of the circumstances binding the government to consignees was the size of its debt, particularly since guano had become the most important part of its fiscal receipts. By 1868 some 18 million pesos were owed for sums advanced to the lessees, while at the same time 50 percent of the government's profit was destined for English bondholders. Inexpertness or, rather, poor administration plus the anxiety to obtain revenue, were significant factors in causing a large part of guano earnings to be used in paying a debt multiplied several times by accumulated interest charges. The some lack of fiscal prudence was responsible for careless negotiations with bondholders of the foreign debt. The same urgency, because of repeated advanced payments, placed the government in a dependent situation with the consignment firms. But the government, contrary to the most prudent advice, depended heavily on guano revenue to defray government expenses. An inflexible short-term fiscal policy which relied heavily on wealth rather than production was evidently condemned to failure.

> Consolidation reached to twenty-three million pesos, nine million of which corresponded to salaries and the rest to confiscations, quotes, embargoes and forced contributions. Echenique adduces that fourteen million in paper was not an exorbitant quantity considering that this covered a period extending from 1820 to 1844 and represented the losses incurred by private individuals during the civil wars as well as international wars and included slaves, livestock, cultivated lands, money, rural property, etc.

And he adds:

> Popular imagination endowed fantastic proportions to the improvisation of fortunes. This attitude is echoed in the text accompanying the word "Consolidation" in Juan de Arona's "Diccionario de Peruanismos." It was the first time that the old forms of social life, more

14 Basadre, *Historia de la República del Perú,* vol. I, p. 230.

or less static even during political upheaval, suffered a severe shake-up. For the first time money emerged as the exclusive social value.

It seems that this injection of capital contributed to forming a new commercial class in Peru and that this was resisted by those who did not participate in the new distribution. What is less evident—or would, at least, have to be determined—is the extent to which this influx of capital, distributed in this manner, had a stimulating effect on the domestic market. That is, how and in what proportions was this income spent. The scandals evolving from consolidation of the domestic debt were an important weapon in creating a mood which culminated in Echenique's fall and in his replacement by a liberal group whose first commitment in 1855 was to abolish slavery. Their liberal spirit did not go to tremendous extremes, and the freeing of the slaves was accompanied by indemnification payments to owners to avoid important social conflicts. These payments were also made out of guano earnings.

Payments to Factors of Production in the Guano Industry

A description of the evolution of the guano industry from 1840 to the end of the 1850s yields the following:

1. Exploitation of guano as a natural resource was initiated by Peruvian entrepreneurs although control of its commercialization process was later transferred to English concessionaires.

2. A considerable portion of the profits was originally to remain inside the country directly in government hands. Nevertheless, of the government's share in earnings, deducting costs (freightage, insurance, and so forth), on which information is lacking but which presumably were considerable, a part was apportioned as follows: (a) to pay bondholders of the debt, (b) indemnifications of the internal debt, which exceeded twenty million pesos, and (c) indemnifications to slave owners.

By demanding advance payments from consignees, the government created the conditions whereby guano exploitation demanded a greater proportion of capital than was actually needed for development, thus making it harder for national companies, obviously

TABLE 2–2 PERUVIAN GOVERNMENT REVENUES
(*in pesos until 1862, in soles thereafter*)

Year	From Guano	Total
1854–1855	4,300,000	9,941,404
1861–1862	16,318,536	20,763,034
1863–1864	18,541,332	23,053,332

SOURCE: Levin, *The Export Economies,* p. 95.

possessing less capital, to compete, despite declarations of parliamentary intent to the contrary.

CONSOLIDATION AND CONVERSION

During the Castilla government several laws had been passed (1847, 1848, and 1850) ordering payment for damages and forced contributions incurred during the War of Independence and in subsequent conflicts. The first two of these laws determined the instances and established proceedings for applying for recognition of claims, while the last declared that recognized claims would be converted into bonds of the domestic public debt paying an annual interest of 6 percent. During the first years claims amounting to 4.3 million pesos were recognized, although in his last message Castilla announced that these would probably rise to 6 or 7 million. The problem of consolidation arose, however, during the following government under Echenique. Under the laws of the preceding government Echenique recognized claims amounting to 19 million pesos, much more, as is evident, than those announced by Castilla. An investigatory committee appointed after the overthrow of Echenique subsequently maintained that at least 12 of those 19 million pesos were paid out to unfounded claims. Echenique himself recognized the objectionable aspects of the system and in 1853 sought from Congress cancellation of all the proceedings. Nevertheless, he maintained that 14 million pesos for the period 1822–1844 was not an exaggerated sum considering how much had been lost in livestock, cultivated lands, dwellings, rural property, and slaves. His purpose in granting claims, however, was apparently different from Castilla's. Jorge Basadre, in reference to consolidation, declared:[15]

> The essential purpose of consolidation was, according to Echenique and his followers, to create national capital and capitalists and thus encourage industry and trade. In the light of such transcendental consequences, what does it matter (asks Echenique in one of his manifestos) if a handful of people became rich if wealth remains in the country and contributes to the realization of these benefits?

Another part corresponds to the lessees, who provided the capital. One can assume that in reality almost all the lessees' profits—around 50 percent—wound up outside the country.

Would this money have remained in the country had guano been exploited by national capital? From our description of Peru's situation in 1840, it appears almost impossible. There was no capital market available within the country. Thus, it was necessary to import capital. The same statement, however, cannot be made for the entire guano period. Not only did the government make the whole process more cumbersome for local capitalists, but once English companies had gained control over the exploitation of guano, they evolved a particular specialization which for a considerable time gave them a virtual monopoly over European distribution of the product. What happened insofar as the other benefits which had been anticipated from the operation within Peru itself? One factor and undoubtedly an important one in this respect is labor. But at the outset of guano development in 1840 could Peru count on the manpower necessary for exploitation of the resource? It must be recalled that at that time:

1. Sixty percent of the Indian population lived in subsistence conditions and did not provide manpower for the labor market.
2. The rigidities of the social structure in the urban sector (guilds) determined its highly immobile characteristics.
3. The part of the population that worked on the plantations existed in conditions verging on slavery or semislavery, so this labor supply was also inelastic.

The lack of manpower was resolved by importing Chinese

[15] Ibid., p. 267.

coolies. While this importation required a high initial capital outlay, it involved workers with a much lower standard of living than the European one, so that salaries were kept extremely low. The number of employees involved in exploitation was high, but cash salaries were minimal and the population existed at a level of infraconsumption.[16] But, on the other hand, the original habits of this labor force were of a very low-level consumption.

Attempts to Employ Guano Earnings to Encourage Development

After the 1840s and 1850s a new generation of Peruvians gradually became aware of the need to utilize more beneficially the resources at their disposal. They reached the conclusion that it was utterly illogical to consume in ordinary expenses (not counting what was spent unwisely) resources which should serve to promote the country's progress. They realized that it was necessary not only to modify the much-criticized system of consignments, but also to channel the profits from guano earnings into more extensive infrastructural projects. Since the railroad at that time constituted a virtual panacea for backwardness, it is not surprising that at the same time as a new guano policy was being proposed two important loans for the construction of a railway system were contracted.

When Balta assumed the presidency and Nicolas de Pierola became minister of the treasury, one of the objectives of government policy was to terminate the consignation system. When guano exploitation was offered to European firms, the only one to accept on the conditions stipulated by the Peruvian government was the Parisian firm of Adolph Dreyfus. On July 5, 1879, a contract was signed which in reality consisted of two separate transactions: first, the purchase and sale of guano, and second, a loan made to the government by the Dreyfus firm for 2 million

16 The distribution of the income that was generated was very unequal and the multiplier effects (demand linkages) scarce.

soles and a subsequent 700,000 pesos annually plus assumption of Peru's foreign debt.

In referring to the Dreyfus contract Basadre maintains:

> For its promoters the Dreyfus contract held many advantages. The country was freed of the dominance of consignees, which led Pierola to refer to the agreement as the Treasury's 2d of May [Independence Day]. Effective service of the foreign debt assured a boost for Peruvian credit. It provided a source for the liquidation of deficits. Guano prices remained high due to the export monopoly. Important economies were introduced into its exploitation and sale. By acquiring a stable income the government could regularize its fiscal expenses, and could secure lower interest rates than those customarily imposed by consignatories.[17]

This contract aroused much resistance among former consignees and among Peruvian capitalists who to some extent felt allied with those who opposed the agreements. This opposition reached the Supreme Court and was successful there, though the Court's decision was ignored in the end by the government.[18]

Nevertheless, even this latter transaction contained certain curious peculiarities. In order to raise capital, Dreyfus issued bonds in international markets which paid a good interest rate of 9 percent plus participation in the guano industry, and, curiously, they were largely subscribed to by Peruvian capital which appeared now as foreign capital. Dreyfus subsequently sold his share in the business to his own company, and when the bondholders appealed for payment, the courts ruled that according to the stipulations of the securities they fell under French jurisdiction. The French court ruled that the Peruvian stockholders would receive payment after all remaining obligations and expenses that Dreyfus had extended to the Peruvian government had been defrayed. The government paid the original sums now multiplied several-fold by interest, huge expenses, and fees, and in the end there was nothing left for

[17] The conversion signified that the internal debt was converted into foreign debt, paying 4 percent instead of 6 percent. The consolidation reached 23 million pesos, 9 million of which were salaries. See Basadre, *Historia de la República del Perú,* vol. II, pp. 39–42.

[18] Basadre says that the contract was a real revolution from above since it attacked powerful interests that were, as may be observed, strongly rooted in Parliament and in the Court. Ibid., p. 45.

Peruvian stockholders, who lost their capital. Earnings from guano sales defrayed interests and capital amortization from loans contracted through the same firm of Dreyfus for construction of the railway line. The initial issue of bonds worth 59.6 million soles was enormously successful (thereby demonstrating the confidence investors had in Peruvian prosperity). In the middle of the investment fever and indebtedness which followed shortly afterward, another loan was taken for 15 million pounds for railroad construction and irrigation works.

The chief railroad lines which crossed the Andean range were established during the great guano boom and in the period immediately following. Later railways either did not cross the mountains or were merely extensions of the trunk lines of 1863 and 1878.

The two trunk lines were the Ferrocarril Central de Lima to the metallurgical centers of La Oraya (and then the mining centers on the Pasco mountains) and the Ferrocarril del Sur from Molendo to Titicaca, passing through Arequipa and extending northwards beyond Cuzco. The aim was to connect the coast with the Sierra, although this accentuated the latter's dependence upon the coast, a result also of the installation of maritime coastal shipping lines replacing the former land communication lines which had united the interior and run parallel to the coast.

In any event, this time, instead of dubious credits, it was guano that financed the railroads, and by 1878 it was possible to say that Peru was ahead of all Latin American countries in terms of railways.

By 1880 guano deposits were nearing depletion. Those on the Chinchas Islands were completely exhausted, while a small amount still remained on the Lobos Islands. At that point, Peru, seeking a substitute field of export, turned its attention to the nitrate deposits in the southern desert zones. The war with Chile signified for Peru the loss of those territories and, for a time, the end of an economy geared chiefly toward export. From 1903–1907 on, copper was the principal export, and it was followed by petroleum, but for a considerable time after 1880 Peru was again an agricultural country relying on its two principal tropical products—sugar and cotton.

Conclusion

Throughout the different vicissitudes which occurred during the period under discussion, Peru developed an export sector which experienced important expansion. What were the characteristics and consequences of this? The location of economic activity was determined by the location of resources. The production was principally resource intensive, although it required also an adequate supply of labor and capital. The government, proprietary of the resource, received the share of earnings derived from the resources. The profits were employed only in a limited degree in infrastructural works, whereas a large portion was used to pay the public debt, war indemnification expenses, commissions, and so forth. With respect to capital, there is no doubt that its earnings were destined to pay those who supplied the capital, the consignatory firms, such as Gibbs and Dreyfus, who organized the operations.

Given the considerable use of labor, one might have anticipated significant distributions of income to that sector. However, the overexploitation of labor prevented a more equitable distribution of income or the likelihood that the effects of this income be extended to any considerable degree.

It is unquestionable, however, that apart from what the government received, mobilization of a large labor force plus development of related activities generated monetary income which undoubtedly made the languishing Peruvian market and particularly its entire urban sector more dynamic. This likewise produced a new commercial class which changed the tenor of the old viceregal city. Though its greatest contribution was the establishment of a railroad network, it must not be forgotten that guano profits also served (1) to eliminate the tribute collected from the Indians, a principal source of fiscal revenue, and (2) to pay for the indemnifications in freeing the slaves. This, in addition to elimination of the rule of primogeniture and of guilds, contributed in a way to modification of the traditional structure of Peruvian society.[19]

[19] Only after this study was completed, Heraclio Bonilla's important study was published: "La coyuntura comercial del siglo XX," *Desarrollo Económico* 12, no. 46 (July–September, 1972): 305–331.

3

CUBA: SUGAR, A PLANTATION ECONOMY

For various reasons the economy of Cuba during the period 1898 to 1930 seems to be the prototypical example of an economy primarily oriented toward export, with that orientation accentuated by monoculture, specialization in the trade of one product, and dependence on virtually a single consumption market. Despite these limitations, Cuban exports exhibited powerful growth as a result of the modernization of its productive structure, which allowed it to compete in international markets. This was achieved largely as a result of incorporating foreign capital and technology plus one additional factor: the labor force that Cuba lacked arrived from other Caribbean areas, such as Jamaica, Yucatán, and even from distant China.

In 1950 the World Bank mission defined this type of economy as follows:

> Few countries are so dependent on international trade as Cuba. In fact, unless it is realized to what extent the island is a one-crop export economy, it is impossible to understand the basic problems of further economic development.
>
> From the end of the 18th century until the middle 1920s free migration, free capital movements and substantially free trade made possible Cuba's spectacular development, along the lines of international specialization.

The World Bank pointed out that the process was more relevant in the 20th century. Not only did more than 600,000 immigrants reach Cuba from Spain, China, and the Caribbean islands, but investments from the United States into Cuba were at least a billion dollars, to which must be added 400 million dollars in bonds negotiated on foreign markets.

> These massive additions to Cuba's labor force and capital powerfully reinforced the natural tendencies which had made the country

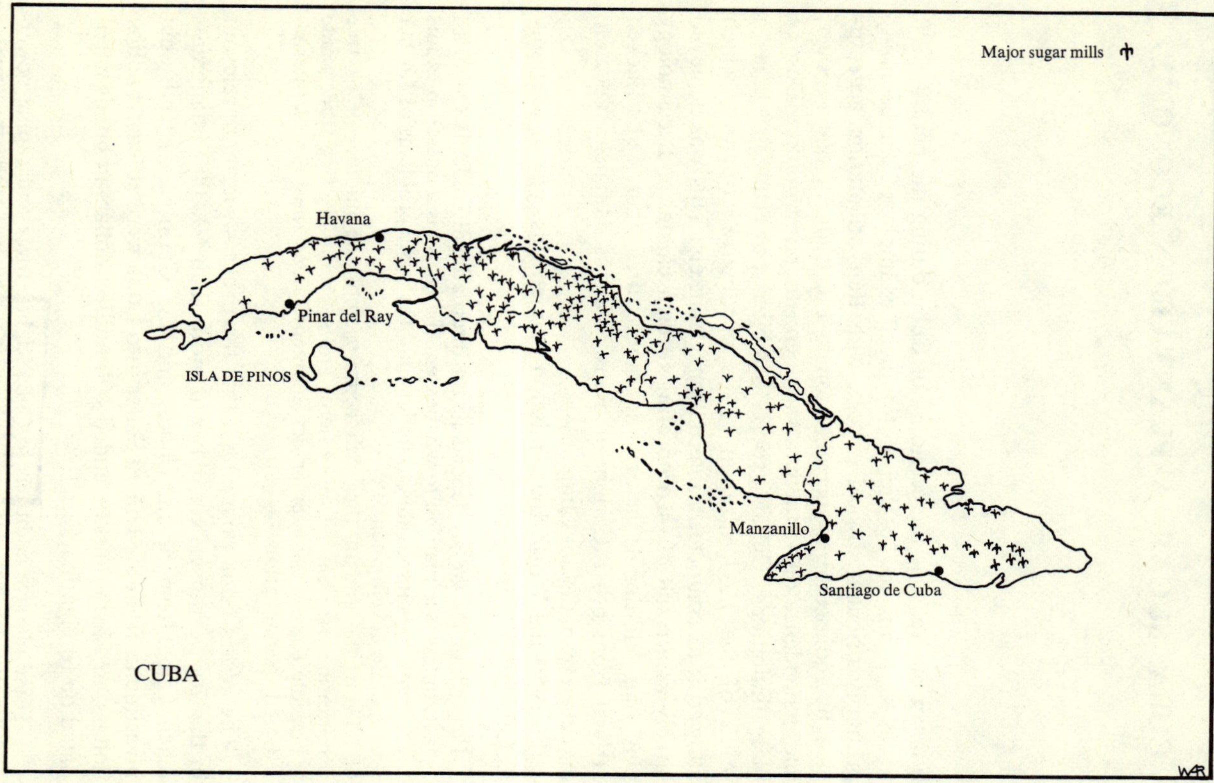

WILLOW ROBERTS

predominantly dependent on foreign trade ever since its early colonial days.

Cuba—the Bank pointed out—was the most important sugar producer in the world. Although it only produced 17 percent of world production, it provided more than 50 percent of the sugar that was sold in the international market. The entire economy was dominated by sugar. It concluded that between a fourth and a third of national income came from sugar production.

> Cuba, though not a monoculture, is nearly so and certainly approaches a mono-export economy. Around 70 percent of Cuba's exports have typically been in the form of sugar products, and in recent years the figure has risen to 90 percent. Since only about 5 percent of her sugar production can be absorbed domestically, Cuba's exports and her large imports of the food, consumer durables, capital equipment and raw materials are linked with the vagaries of the world's sugar markets.
>
> Domestic prosperity thus depends upon forces beyond the nation's control and changes in the price of sugar or in its market outlets make the difference between well-being and depression.[1]

The *latifundio,* the concentration of the sugar industry in a few sugar mills, nearly total dependence on this export product and therefore on the fluctuations of international demand and prices, subordination to foreign capital, the existence of a developed urban sector alongside an impoverished rural sector have been familiar conditions to Cubans for a long time.[2] In recent decades they have reached the status of clichés—subjects disseminated by mass media throughout the world.

Cuba, however, had not always been a country whose economy was nearly totally oriented toward a plantation type export. It is well known that the extension of the cultivation of sugar, which had been brought by Columbus in his second voyage to Española and from there to Cuba by Diego de Velázquez at the beginning of its colonization, was relatively unsuccessful. At that time the Span-

[1] International Bank for Reconstruction and Development: *Report on Cuba* (Baltimore, Md.: Johns Hopkins Press, 1951), pp. 194, 195, 723.

[2] Concerning this see the pioneer work of Ramiro Guerra y Sánchez, *Azúcar y población en las Antillas* (Havana: Cultural S.A., 1944). English version: *Sugar and Society in the Caribbean: An Economic History of Cuban Agriculture* (New Haven, Conn.: Yale University Press, 1964).

iards, in the initial phase of their colonial enterprise in the islands, were interested in the exploitation of metallic wealth, principally gold, which was found in riverbeds.[3] When this was depleted they sought new sources of income elsewhere—Mexico, Florida, and Peru. The result was an extremely unstable form of colonization. Precarious villages functioned as long as a resource was exploited, whereupon it was abandoned in quest of another. In Cuba the rapid depletion of minerals and, especially, the early decline of the Indian population, which left the Spanish colonizers without a source of resources, tribute, and labor supply, accentuated this process. This marked the conclusion of the insular phase of Spanish colonization in America.[4]

Sugar, which was known early in Cuba, did not enjoy the same success that it did in Brazil, precisely because Cuba lacked the conditions—primarily a labor supply—that made its exploitation possible in the Portuguese colony.[5] Whereas Portugal had specialized in navigation along the East African coast, which was extremely close to northeastern Brazil, and therefore was in a position to search for and import slave labor from Africa, the Spanish colonizers lacked that same possibility at the very time when they were confronted with a sudden decline of the Indian population (which furthermore was ill-suited to plantation work). Whereas the association of the Dutch and Portuguese furnished relatively large sums of capital from the onset of the operation and also channels for commercializing the product in Europe, the same was not the case with the Spaniards. And, finally, the Portuguese possessed a special know-how in sugar production which others lacked.[6] Because of these circumstances, despite its suitable land

[3] See John Parry, *The Spanish Seaborne Empire* (New York: Alfred A. Knopf, 1967).

[4] See Carl Sauer, *The Early Spanish Main* (Berkeley and Los Angeles, Calif.: University of California Press, 1966) and Charles Gibson, *Spain in America* (New York: Harper & Row, 1966).

[5] Robert P. Porter, *Industrial Cuba* (New York: G. P. Putnam Sons, The Knickerbocker Press, 1899), p. 281. Porter says, "Although it made so early a start in the history of American agriculture, the sugar industry in Cuba languished for two hundred years."

[6] Celso Furtado, *The Economic Growth of Brazil* (Berkeley and Los Angeles, Calif.: University of California Press, 1963).

and favorable climate, Cuba did not develop a plantation economy in the earliest colonial period but rather a totally different agrarian organization of free *colonos*. Given the relationship of existing resources, abundant lands and scarce population, the prevalent form of agrarian development was extensive cattle raising. The *hacienda,* therefore, was more the result of the factors of production existing in Cuba at that time than of legal norms. Although this permitted the development of a group of landowners of large- and medium-sized holdings, the origins of modern latifundio are not to be found in this structure. There is a simple reason for this: properties were large because there was great abundance of land and, hence, their value was almost nil.

The very need to maintain an adequate size for this type of exploitation led to a most curious phenomenon—the formation of the *comunal hacienda*. These lands were owned in common by various landholders (all descendants of a single original owner), who could not divide the land among themselves but instead distributed titles (a kind of shares) to the property which were called *pesos de posesión* (possession pesos).[7] These communal holders, however, owned their cattle individually and had them branded for purposes of identification. Only in the nineteenth century, as wealth increased with the beginning of tobacco cultivation and then that of sugar, did the demand for land increase and the dissolution of the communal hacienda occur. During the entire seventeenth century (a period of general decline in the whole Spanish empire)[8] and for a large part of the eighteenth century the Cuban economy was devoted to cattle raising. In addition to the class of large- and medium-sized cattle ranchers, descendants of the colonizers and rooted to the soil, there also existed a rather prosperous

[7] Concessions were granted in circular farms (*estancias*), larger farms (*hatos*) and corrals. A description of the appropriation process and the division of land in Cuba can be found in Guerra, *Azúcar y población en las Antillas.* Julio le Riverand has also discussed this topic in *Los orígenes de la economía cubana, 1510–1600,* Jornada no. 46 (Mexico City: El Colegio de México, 1945), chap. 2. See also Franklin W. Knight, *Slave Society in Cuba during the Nineteenth Century* (Madison, Wisc.: University of Wisconsin Press, 1970), pp. 3–46.

[8] See Woodrow Borah, "New Spain's Century of Depression," *Iberoamericana* 35 (June 1951).

urban sector whose income derived from the semiannual arrival of fleets in Havana. The seasonal nature of this activity, however, produced marked imbalances: strong inflationary pressures during the fleet's stay and prolonged depressions in its absence.

Antedating the cultivation of sugar was that of tobacco in the eastern provinces of Cuba (Pinar del Río, Santiago de Cuba), for tobacco required less capital and a smaller labor supply. Tobacco was tilled in fairly limited strips of land, or *vegas,* bordering rivers, and it, unlike a slave-based crop (the usual plantation type economy), required rather skilled labor rather than large numbers of workers. Tobacco at that point was the agricultural export crop of the free worker who owned his own land. This fact is of prime importance in all of Cuba's subsequent political history. The form of crop distribution also determined the early population movements toward the interior, following the rivers.[9]

In 1703 marketing the crop was placed under Spanish government monopoly with the creation of the tobacco *estanco*. Later on, well into the period of tobacco expansion, the Royal Trade Company was organized to administer the distribution process. Tobacco exports rose between 1760 and 1800 from an annual average of about 10,000 *arrobas* to about 100,000. Growth was much greater in the nineteenth century. In 1845, 298,000 arrobas were exported and in 1850, 346,000.[10]

Meanwhile, the cultivation of sugar, limited by a lack of capital and labor, remained at a low level. Slave labor, one must realize, was extremely costly during the colonial period because of duties imposed on the importation of slaves by the Spanish crown. Two episodes produced brief booms in the slave trade and contributed to the expansion of sugar cultivation. These were, first, the settlement permission granted to the British in 1715, a concession that was made as a result of the Treaty of Utrecht and not maintained very long; and, second, free entry of slaves during the months of

[9] Tobacco undoubtedly requires a larger labor force than extensive cattle raising. The degree to which tobacco extends into former cattle regions also depends on those regions being populated.

[10] The Cuban Economic Research Project, University of Miami, *A Study on Cuba: The Cuban Economic Research Project* (Coral Gables, Fla.: University of Miami Press, 1965), p. 73.

the English occupation from August 1762 to July 1763. The latter was an important precedent invoked by the colonos in order to obtain reduced import duties on laborers. In 1789 the Spanish authorities at last granted a two-year permission period for the free entry of slaves which was eventually prolonged at the insistence of the planters who had plunged into the cultivation of sugar cane. During that same period a totally external circumstance furnished an additional and important incentive. The impact in Haiti of the French Revolution led the slave population to rise against colonial domination. The black revolution cost not only many lives among the white population, but also the massive destruction of sugar plantations, a symbol of the denigrating slavery to which blacks had been condemned. The disappearance of Haitian production, in conjunction with that of the British Indies, the principal producers at that time, was strongly felt in a decline of total production, causing thereby a steep rise in prices. Furthermore, as is usually the case in such instances, there was a pronounced flight of capital from these besieged areas. A considerable number of French planters transferred their capital to Cuba.[11] Free slave trade in 1818 at last provided the necessary resources for stimulating production.

Cuban sugar exports rose in the manner recorded in Table 3–1.

Labor availability, the freeing of trade, the opening of new markets, a rise in prices, and entry of capital were factors that provided a strong impetus to sugar activity. At first, that is, to about 1820, this was not accomplished on any large scale with

[11] *Problems of the New Cuba: Report of the Commission on Cuban Affairs* (New York: The Foreign Policy Assoc. Co., 1935), chap. 10, p. 218.

Sugar cane was brought to Cuba by its first Governor, Diego Velasquez, in the second decade of the sixteenth century. It began to be manufactured in small quantities for export toward the end of that century. But the amount was trivial until the stimulus given commerce by the British occupation of Havana in 1762. This impetus was reinforced after 1791 by the civil wars in Haiti, which eliminated the leading sugar-producing area in the world, and transferred many French planters to Cuba. During the Napoleonic period, Cuban ports became open to foreign merchants, encouragement was given to the importation of slaves and to the colonization of immigrants, and Cuban producers were able to take advantage of the favorable development of the market for sugar in the United States and Great Britain.

TABLE 3–1 CUBAN SUGAR EXPORTS ACCORDING TO PEZUELA AND HUMBOLDT

Years	Pezuela (millions of arrobas)	Humboldt (crates)[a]
1550–1599	0.02	—
1601–1699	0.04	—
1700–1753	0.16	—
1754–1760	0.20	—
1761–1763	0.39	13,000[b]
1764–1769	1.21	—
1770–1778	8.60	50,000
1779–1785	9.80	—
1786–1790	5.45	340,661
1791–1795	7.57	419,904
1796–1800	11.46	719,878
1801–1805	14.82	990,817
1806–1810	15.10	890,171
1811–1815	14.49	1,040,059
1816–1820	18.05	1,033,277
1821–1824	20.02	1,044,004
1825	4.49	488,776[c]
1826–1830	32.54	2,433,793
1831–1835	39.46	2,436,492
1836–1840	50.74	3,171,423
1841–1845	64.33	4,024,405
1846–1850	93.45	4,340,768

[a] *According to José García de Arboleya,* Manual de Historia de Cuba, *2d ed.* (*Havana: Imprenta del Tiempo, 1859*), *p. 245, one crate of sugar contained from seventeen to twenty-two arrobas. Guerra,* in Azúcar y población en las Antillas, *p. 225, quoting Uxtariz,* Técnica y práctica del comercio, *indicates that a crate contained forty arrobas, but that this was true during the sixteenth and part of the seventeenth centuries; hence, the unit employed is that indicated by García de Arboleya, since it allows comparing the crate statistics given by Humboldt and Pezuela.*

[b] *This figure given by Humboldt corresponds to the years 1760–1763.*

[c] *From 1825 to 1850 the figures are the official ones compiled by Thrashea in the English edition of Humboldt's book. Humboldt was the first to publish statistics on the annual export of sugar through the port of Havana up to 1824, his data were used by La Sagra and later by Pezuela.*

SOURCE: The Cuban Economic Research Project, University of Miami, *A Study on Cuba* (Coral Gables, Fla.: University of Miami Press, 1965), p. 180. Statistics from Jacobo de la Pezuela, *Diccionario Geográfico, Estadístico. Histórico de la Isla de Cuba,* vol. II (Madrid: Imprenta del Establecimiento Mellado e Imprenta del Banco Industrial y Mercantil, 1863–1866), pp. 61–63; Alejandro de Humboldt, *Ensayo político sobre la Isla de Cuba* (Havana: Cultural S.A., 1930).

TABLE 3–2 COFFEE EXPORTS
(*in millions and fractions of arrobas*)

1805	0.1
1810	0.4
1815	0.9
1820	0.9
1825	1.0
1830	1.8
1840	2.1
1845	0.6
1850	0.5
1860	0.7
1867	0.2

SOURCE: The Cuban Economic Research Project, *A Study on Cuba*, p. 75.

companies that employed a great number of laborers and extensive capital. It was the result, rather, of an increase in the area under cultivation with a more or less restricted and limited use of labor—numerous units employing a limited number of workers per unit. Though this permitted a more equitable distribution of wealth, it also is certain that this type of production was less efficient.

The first period of growth lasted until the 1820s when sugar was replaced to a significant degree by coffee, which became the principal export product.

The rise in coffee production is also linked to the immigration of French planters who fled from Haiti. Though its production between 1810 and 1840 grew five-fold, it expanded no further. The Spanish government's fiscal policy and the measures adopted by other countries against Cuban coffee in retaliation to Spain's trade policy were among the factors responsible for the decline of coffee. As coffee declined, sugar regained its importance, which had not been lost completely. As Porter noted:

> From 1840 to 1850, the production of sugar increased gradually from 200,000 to about 300,000 tons. Prices of coffee began to decline owing to excess of production and competition of Brazil, and

all the attention was given to cane growing, so much so that from 1853 to 1868, the production was rapidly increased to the following figures:

1853	322,000 tons	1861	466,000 tons
1854	374,000 tons	1862	525,000 tons
1855	392,000 tons	1863	507,000 tons
1856	348,000 tons	1864	575,000 tons
1857	355,000 tons	1865	620,000 tons
1858	385,000 tons	1866	612,000 tons
1859	536,000 tons	1867	597,000 tons
1860	447,000 tons	1868	749,000 tons

This period of sixteen years was really the so-called Golden Age of Cuba.[12]

Table 3–3 indicates the relationship between the rise in production and the number of mills in the country between the end of the eighteenth century and 1850.

Although total production increased faster than the number of mills (the average mill produced 30 tons in 1792, 46 tons in 1802, 90 tons in 1827, and 200 tons in 1850), no trend toward concentration was yet apparent. In fact, expansion was based primarily on the incorporation of new units of production. In the years that followed, the number of small sugar mills continued to increase and in 1860 reached 2,000.

Despite the steady growth of sugar production, the industry, starting in the fifties and even in the sixties, faced serious problems. In order to overcome them a substantial modification in the organization of production was necessary, and when this was accomplished, the industry acquired its present modern configuration. One of its principal difficulties was competition with beet sugar in the European and North American markets. In 1853 beet sugar represented only 13.7 percent of the world sugar market; in 1862 it had risen to 31.2 percent. The fall in world demand, due to this increase in beet sugar production, caused an abrupt decline in prices. With respect to this decline Porter notes:

> As a cane-sugar producing country, nature has made Cuba superior to any competitor which may appear; but all sugar does not come from cane and since 1840, when the first record of beet sugar appeared, with 50,000 tons for the year's output for the world, as

[12] Porter, *Industrial Cuba*, pp. 291 and 292.

TABLE 3–3 NUMBER OF MILLS AND TOTAL PRODUCTION OF SUGAR

Years	Mills	Production (in thousands of tons)	Production (per mill in tons)
1792	473	14	30
1802	870	40	46
1827	1,000	90	90
1850	1,500	300	200

SOURCE: Leland H. Jenks, *Our Cuban Colony* (New York: The Vanguard Press, 1928), p. 25.

against 1,100,000 tons of cane sugar, about 200,000 tons of which was raised in Cuba, the sugar growers of the Island have had their only dangerous rival. Beginning with the small production of 50,000 tons in 1840, principally grown in France, the beet sugar production increased rapidly in Europe, reaching 200,000 tons in 1850; 400,000 tons in 1860, 900,000 tons in 1870; 1,860,000 tons in 1880; and in 1894 going to 3,841,000 tons.[13]

This already difficult situation was further aggravated by the following factors:

1. The inefficient use of labor in an economy with scarce labor, a situation exacerbated by the fact that the slave trade was increasingly costly. Lack of a labor supply impelled a totally different approach than that reached after the belated liberation of the slaves on February 13, 1880.[14]

2. The limited availability of land. The sugar expansion during this initial period was effected through the addition of new cultivated areas. These lands, however, were not unlimited.

3. The crises in European and North American markets in 1857 and 1866 extended to Cuba and affected numerous operations which had assumed financial obligations in earlier boom periods

[13] Ibid., pp. 282 and 283.

[14] Although, in fact, in 1878 slavery lacked the importance it had before the Ten Years War, the mills operated under very different conditions with at times 40 percent slave labor and varying proportions of free labor. Cf. Julio le Riverand, "Historia Económica," book IV, in Guerra et al. eds. *Historia de la Nación Cubana* (Havana: Ed. Historia de la Nación Cubana, 1952), vol. 7, p. 179.

that fell in periods of financial stress and low prices, leading numerous small operations into ruin.

By the 1860s the sugar industry had reached a point at which expansion under previous conditions of exploitation came to a halt. The Ten Years War (1868–1878) also contributed to the elimination of the less vigorous operations which were unable to withstand the economic consequences of depredation, conflicts, and crises. Later on, recovery was characterized by the depression and extension of sugar cultivation.[15]

The New Organization of the Sugar Industry from 1880 to the End of the Century

The new phase of the sugar industry was characterized by conditions that distinguished it from the earlier period.

1. Evolution of an industrial organization marked by a division of labor between the mill and the cane producer. The numerous small mills where the producer himself refined the cane were eliminated. Then there appeared *centrales* equipped with more capital, which allowed for more efficient production. The centrales would later control by other means the colono's production, and the latter became simply a sharecropper. Although initially the concentration of property was not a characteristic feature, it developed later from the centrales' need of securing for themselves a supply of raw material. Property was acquired in order to control the colono's production. This led to the concentration of property and the latifundio, a process also favored by the other features of this new phase of production.[16]

[15] *Problems of the New Cuba,* p. 219.

But the installation of improved machinery meant increased capital outlays, and it became evident that the larger enterprises had numerous production advantages. These tendencies toward concentration which appeared in the sixties were consequently resumed with more rapid tempo after the "Ten Years War."

[16] By the early nineties there were only four-hundred-odd mills still grinding, averaging some 1,500 tons, nearly 10,000 bags a piece. This concentration was hastened by the catastrophic fall in the price of sugar due to the rise of bountiful beet sugar in Central Europe, which rapidly eliminated marginal plantations in favor of those whose mechanical efficiency enabled

TABLE 3–4 NUMBER OF MILLS, 1846 AND 1890

1846	1,442
1890	400

SOURCE: *Problems of the New Cuba,* pp. 218 and 219.

TABLE 3–5 PRODUCTION, 1853, 1868, AND 1894

1853	322,000 tons
1868	749,000 tons
1894	1,054,214 tons

SOURCE: Porter, *Industrial Cuba,* pp. 291 and 293.

2. The establishment of a railroad system enabled the development of new lands in more remote areas and also encouraged a strong dependence of the producer on the central, who generally owned the railroad.

them to extract two or three times as much sugar from the cane. It was also furthered by the uncompensated emancipation of slaves in Cuba, and ensuing agricultural adjustments. In this process a large number of estates passed into the hands of newcomers from the Spanish Peninsula, many of them originally merchants, while Cuban planters, large and small, became attached to the new centrales under contract as colonos, devoting themselves entirely to the raising of cane.

The Wilson Tariff of 1894 and the Cuban revolution hastened the process of elimination and concentration. When the industry began to revive in 1904 under the aegis of American reciprocity, there were only 173 mills grinding, with a total output of 1,040,228 tons. This made the average output per mill about 41,000 bags. The industry now grew steadily at rates even more rapid than those which prevailed in the early nineteenth century. The expansion was almost entirely in the mechanical capacity of individual mills and in more extensive cane zones, which meant at first an increasing proportion of colono cane as compared with administration cane grown directly by the mill itself. Ibid., p. 219. See also Guerra, *Azúcar y población en las Antillas,* pp. 93 et seq.

3. The massive importation of free or semifree labor to replace slaves. The famous *contratados,* or contracted laborers, who came from Yucatán, Jamaica, and finally, China.

The new structure of the industry corresponded to an increasing concentration of fewer mills and, on the other hand, to a significant rise in production.

Perhaps the most significant factor in this modernization process of the industry was the division of labor between mill and producer. The Report of the Commission on Cuban Affairs described the system of the central and colonos as follows:

> The predominating mode of organizing agricultural activities in Cuba is what is known as the colono system, which in various forms is wide-spread in sugar-producing countries. Under this system the agricultural risks, with exception of those involving variability in the sugar content of the cane, are assumed by a cane planter who undertakes to sell this cane to the mill in return for a stipulated portion of the raw sugar produced from it. This system arose in Cuba in the eighties and nineties, partly as a means for providing field labor, and partly as a device to relieve mills of financial burdens in the period of transition from the plantation system to modern factories. The relations of colonos with the centrales have always exhibited great diversity, and most mills have at all times raised some cane for themselves under what is known as the administration system. Moreover, while some colonos grow cane on their land, the larger number use land owned by or leased on behalf of the central. The degree to which these different field systems prevail on any given estate seems to depend chiefly on original conditions of land tenure and the availability of cane. In the older provinces of the island there were a great many holdings, and with the reorganization of the sugar industry after the Ten Years' War the owners of many of these planted cane to secure a cash crop. Many centrales are the result of a concentration about a single producing unit of a number of old plantations. Many plantation owners thus became colonos to large centrales. On the other hand, where the central developed out of a plantation, it already had some cane land at its disposal which it was usually convenient to operate under the administration system.
>
> Moreover, many mills maintain some administration cane for experimental purposes. Competition for cane in areas crowded with mills has also promoted steps to bring it under mill control. With the rise of sugar production at the eastern end of the island in new areas another situation presented itself. Companies bought land in large tracts and found it convenient to grant much of it on lease to farmers and others with capital who undertook the work of clearing the land and assisted in recruiting the necessary field labor. Each of

these types has spread to mills where other situations existed, and there have been changes from time to time in their respective roles in the raising of cane.[17]

Among other things, the division of labor between mill and producer was a prerequisite for the investment of substantial capital, which, in turn, contributed to the technological modernization of the industry creating the conditions necessary for efficient operation.[18]

There were, however, other important factors in the expansion of the sugar industry and they are discussed below.

The North American Sugar Market and the Investment of North American Capital

Trade between Cuba and the United States seems almost a geographic imperative, so close is the island to the coasts of Florida. The interest of the United States in Cuba dates from the beginning of the nineteenth century.[19] During the time in which the island was under Spanish rule, while revolutionary conflicts extended throughout the old empire, there were several annexation attempts made by the United States as well as by Cubans themselves. These attempts were linked to a large extent to attempts made by the island's planters to maintain the slave trade, which was threatened

[17] *Problems of the New Cuba,* p. 270. Incomplete returns for 1904–1905 show 30.3 percent of the cane area under administration, 33.2 percent operated by colonos on mill land, and 36.5 percent operated by colonos on their own land-independent colonos.

[18] This period marked the incorporation of production factors from abroad which Cuba lacked—labor and capital. This lack was a permanent obstacle for the expansion of the sugar industry.

[19] John Quincy Adams's opinion on the importance of Cuba is given by Arthur Whitaker in *Los Estados Unidos y la independencia de América Latina* (Buenos Aires: Eudeba, 1964), p. 26. "Thus Cuba, which can be seen from our beaches, has become, due to a multitude of considerations, an object of transcendental importance for the political and commercial interests of our Union," Adams wrote in April 1823. English version: *The United States and the Independence of Latin America, 1800–1830* (Baltimore, Md.: The Johns Hopkins Press, 1941). See also Lester D. Langley, *The Cuban Policy of the United States: A Brief History* (New York: Wiley, 1968).

by restrictions agreed upon by Great Britain and Spain (particularly the prohibition of trafficking in blacks). Reactions in the United States varied according to the individual state's position toward slavery. There was even a purchasing offer made by the United States and rejected by Spain, as well as other attempts, which, though less legal, were not therefore more veiled. The Civil War in the United States brought to an end a period in which Cuba was regarded as likely to follow Texas's example and become a state.[20]

Although these attempts failed and, prior to the war with Spain and the military occupation of Cuba, the United States did not intervene directly in Cuban affairs, the entrance of North American capital predates the war. There is no doubt, however, that the Platt Amendment imposed on the newly independent Cuban nation by its benefactor, the United States, was the most decisive factor in directing a strong flow of capital toward the island. The first investments of North American capital were made in the railroads, though they were subsequently exceeded by English investments.[21]

In the sugar industry United States investments were made through various channels, though finance was the one most frequently used. This is the case of the Boston firm, E. Atkins and Company, which acquired the property of the Sarría family in 1893. The Sarrías had operated the Soledad plantation since 1833, which included about 13,000 acres, twenty-three mills, and its own railway. During the reorganization of the industry during the nineteenth century, the Sarría operation assumed numerous obligations in order to acquire equipment and capital goods, thus incurring debts which, in a period of crisis and declining prices, they were unable to meet. The firm of Atkins, their principal creditor, thus gained ownership of the Soledad refinery which had belonged to the Sarrías. Another example is that of Robert Bradley

20 Regarding annexation attempts, see R. Guerra, *Manual de Historia Cubana* (Havana: Editora Universitaria, 1964), chaps. 18, 19, and 20; Philip S. Foner, *A History of Cuba and Its Relations with the United States,* vol. 2, 1845–1895 (New York: International Publishers, 1963), chaps. 1 and 2; and Langley, *The Cuban Policy of the United States.*

21 Concerning the beginning of North American investments, see *Problems of the New Cuba,* pp. 219–220.

Hawley, a Congressman from Texas with strong interests in Louisiana's beet sugar industry. The collection of unpaid debts incurred through credits resulted in the transfer of Mario Menocal's property, perhaps the most important on the island, constituting 60,000 acres and a production capacity equal to 10 percent of the total Cuban output. Once the transfer was made, Menocal remained in charge of the company (renamed the Cuban-American Sugar Company) as administrator of Hawley's interests. In reference to this, the economic historian Julio le Riverand remarked that sugar expansion in Cuba ought to be regarded as a continuation of the industry's expansion (especially that of beet sugar) in the United States (Louisiana). North American sugar producers who had integrated the process of primary production with that of sugar refining were in need of raw material to maintain their refineries in full operation.[22]

Though these were the initial steps in the establishment of United States influence in Cuba, the decisive elements in the close relationship binding Cuba to the United States were added after the war with Spain: on the one hand, the Platt Amendment, and on the other, the tariff reductions on trade arising from the application of the Reciprocal Trade Agreement. While sugar prices were continuing on their downward slope, a bill was presented to the United States Congress which would authorize the president to reduce the import tariff on all Cuban merchandise by 20 percent if Cuba would grant the same preference to the United States. The proposal, which aroused considerable opposition in Congress, was subsequently approved and incorporated as part of the Reciprocal Trade Agreement of 1902. The end of resistance to the importation of raw sugar cane signified for many the union of the sugar trust with beet sugar interests in the United States. In this manner sugar trade destined for the United States not only increased but became almost totally oriented toward the United States.

> Until 1909 practically all of Cuban sugar exports were sent to the United States, although Cuban sugar was far from constituting the total amount of sugar imported by the United States. After that date

22 See Julio le Riverand, in Guerra, *Historia de la Nación Cubana,* p. 312. This also explains the tariff situation. See Philip G. Wright, *The Cuban Situation and Our Treaty Relations* (Washington, D.C.: The Foreign Policy Association, 1931), p. 63.

TABLE 3–6 ESTIMATED VALUES OF DIRECT UNITED STATES INVESTMENTS IN CUBA

Years	Millions of Dollars
Before 1894	50
1898–1902	30
1902–1906	80
1929	919

SOURCE: Jenks, *Our Cuban Colony,* p. 162, and, for 1929, IBRD, *Report on Cuba,* p. 732.

the Cuban share in the United States market increased from representing 69.7 percent in 1909 to 99.1 percent in 1925 (in 1900 it was 20.8 percent and in 1905, 57.1 percent; in 1909, 69.7 percent). The United States continued as the principal consumer of Cuban sugar (in proportions oscillating from 100 percent in 1909 to 77.9 percent in 1929).[23]

Until 1909 practically all of Cuba's increased production was absorbed by the expanding American market. In 1914 the United States still took 86.7 percent of Cuba's supplies and had virtually ceased to import sugar paying full duty. As Cuban production further expanded, it became increasingly dependent on the hazards of the world market.[24]

The tariff reduction meant better prices for the producer. On the other hand, during periods of surplus production, it accentuated the depressed price trend. Once the North American market was supplied, the producer was forced to take his surplus to European markets, London and Hamburg, where the same preference did not exist and where he had to sell at lower prices. Hence, although prices were going down, he tried to continue selling in the New York market, at least while he could obtain a difference in the tariffs. This market pressure tended to reduce the average price of sugar. In the end, this worked to the benefit of sugar refiners who obtained imported raw material at lower prices. The importation of *already* refined sugar, however, did not enjoy the same prefer-

[23] Wright, *The Cuban Situation,* pp. 59 and 65; and *A Study on Cuba,* pp. 244 and 245.

[24] *Problems of the New Cuba,* p. 220.

FIGURE 3–1 AVERAGE OUTPUT OF CUBAN SUGAR MILLS, 1904–1933, MEDIAN OUTPUT, 1923–1933

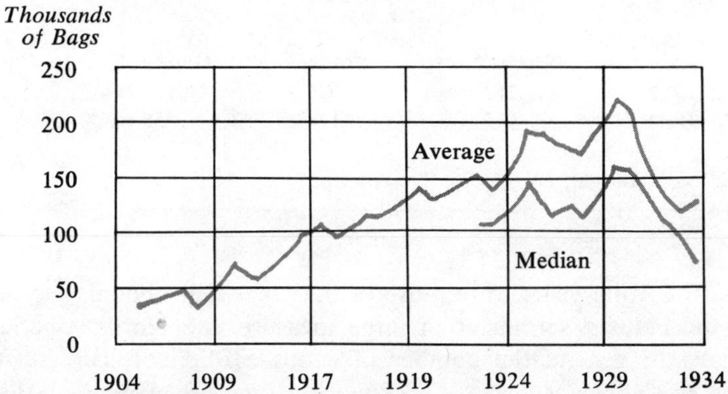

SOURCE: *Problems of the New Cuba,* p. 220.

ence. All of these circumstances contributed to increasing the incorporation of North American capital, even among properties belonging to the sugar trust. Table 3–6 illustrates the progression of North American capital investments in Cuba.

Toward the end of the last century those who started the chain of American investors were E. Atkins and Company, owners of the Soledad mill; Hugh Kelly and Franklin Farrel, founders of Santa Teresa; and the Rionada group, who owned the Tuinucua Cane Sugar Company. Around 1906 the United States investment in the sugar industry was calculated at 30 million dollars; in 1911, at 50 million; and it continued to rise rapidly. Actually the transfer of most of the sugar industry into North American possession occurred as a result of the collapse following the boom of the 1920s.

The concentration and greater investments of capital were translated into an increase in the productivity of each mill.

Shortly before World War I 25 percent of the capital invested in the sugar industry was North American. In 1920 production had doubled and 48.4 percent was with North American capital.[25]

[25] Wright, *The Cuban Situation,* p. 57. Production reaches 5 million tons while 75 percent is North American property.

TABLE 3–7 PRODUCTION OF BEET SUGAR IN VARIOUS EUROPEAN COUNTRIES
(*in thousands of tons*)

	Germany	France	Austria-Hungary	Russia
1912–1913	3,012	1,079	2,166	1,550
1919–1920	815	170	558	97

SOURCE: Wright, *The Cuban Situation,* p. 71.

The following years were those of the great sugar boom, and also of the industry's transfer in large measure into North American hands. In general the number of centrales did not increase. Of greater significance was the expansion and broadening of those already in existance.

THE EXCEPTIONAL BOOM OF THE 1920S AND THE SUBSEQUENT CRISIS

World War I and its ensuing consequences rid Cuban sugar of one of its most dangerous competitors—European beet sugar. The elimination of competition was translated into a phenomenal rise in prices which served as an important incentive for increasing production and for stimulating investments in the industry, which permitted increasing yields.[26]

All of this induced an investment craze which dissolved in the crisis of 1921. Prices, which had soared from 1.95 cents in 1913 to the incredible level of 20 cents a pound in the month of May 1920, dropped rapidly. Markets were oversaturated. Cuba still retained part of its unsold sugar stock from the previous year. European fields of beet sugar were rehabilitated. The price decline was tremendous. Prices never again rose to the 1919 and 1920 levels and later were to suffer the disastrous effects of the 1929 crisis.

[26] See investment graph in *Problems of the New Cuba,* p. 222.

TABLE 3–8 SUGAR PRICES

	(U.S. cents per pound)
1913	1.95
1914	2.64
1915	3.31
1916	4.37
1918	4.24
1919	5.06
1920	11.95

SOURCE: Secretaría de Agricultura, Comercio y Trabajo, *Industria Azucarera Zafra de 1930*, p. 109, cited by Wright, *The Cuban Situation*, p. 54.

Having contracted excessive debts as a result of the promise of easy earnings, many of the entrepreneurs and, of course, those with less capital, primarily Cubans and Spaniards, were unable to withstand the collapse and surrendered their properties in order to pay their mortages.

The report of the Commission on Cuban Affairs describes the situation as follows:

> The United States ended its sugar control suddenly, toward the end of 1910, and sugar soared for the few delirious months of the "Dance of the Millions." The invisible sugars began to appear, and prices fell even more rapidly than they had risen. The ensuing crisis came at a moment when large numbers of mills were heavily involved in new plantings, and had made new machinery installations at inflated prices. It coincided, moreover, with a bank crisis which destroyed the bulk of the local banking institutions. Under these circumstances liquidation meant the rapid transfer of large numbers of properties into the possession of Americans, especially American banks and corporations whose own difficulties were giving those banks a decisive voice in their affairs.
>
> The financing of a nineteenth century sugar plantation was simple. The planter simply bought the place with his own accumulated funds or paid something down and gave a mortgage on the rest, which he rapidly retired out of earnings. Dead season and crop activities were financed, when necessary, by sugar merchants who contracted to market the sugar when it was made. As the normal size of mills has grown, however, the earlier modes of long-term financing have be-

TABLE 3–9 SUGAR PRICES, 1920–1930

	(U.S. cents per pound)
1920	11.95
1921	3.03
1922	2.77
1923	4.98
1924	3.85
1925	2.26
1926	2.30
1927	2.67
1928	2.20
1929	1.73
1930	1.25

SOURCE: U.S. Tariff Commission, cited by Wright, *The Cuban Situation,* p. 771.

come impossible for all but a very few mill-owners, and new agencies have absorbed most of the business of financing the crop.

At the present time all but about thirty of the mills in Cuba are owned by corporate enterprises of one kind or another. The stock of most of the rest is owned by comparatively few individuals. During the twenties, however, there was a tendency for many of the companies to appeal to a wider investing public by public offerings of bonds and in some cases, of stock. This was particularly true of companies which came under the control of great American banks and security houses.

The activity of North American banks in the sugar business, however, did not start with these long-term financial operations. One of the most useful functions of the Banco Nacional, which was closed in 1921, was to begin the process of taking away crop financing from the sugar merchants. As North American banks extended their branches into Cuba they competed actively for this business and have absorbed the bulk of it since the failure of local banks.

It was through their involvements in crop financing and loans for new plantings that the commercial banks were chiefly drawn into the problems of long-term financing, especially after the crisis of 1921. It is correct to say that in many cases they made fresh loans, facilitating expansion, to protect previous advances. It is not correct, however, to infer from this that many New York banks, caught up in the enthusiasm of the Coolidge era, did not go into this business with eagerness. They bought properties to combine with those which had come into their hands through foreclosure, and issued securities

> on them which they pressed enthusiastically on their investment clientele. Bankers, as well as investors, have come to regard this activity as unfortunate. The resulting over-expansion of the sugar industry, the concentration of labor and capital in places where no sugar mills should have been erected, the depletion of large areas of virgin forest, and the ruthless business tactics employed by some bank-dominated concerns have left the Cuban people a sorry recollection of the entry of the banks into the sugar business.[27]

The industry was thus transferred in many instances from producers to the banks that were the principal creditors. The First National City Bank of New York became one of the most important investors in the sugar business. The difficult situation that sugar producers were going through was further aggravated by the emergency tariff passed in the United States which raised the duty on Cuban sugar from 1 cent per pound to 1.6 cents (a 60 percent increase). While the weakest producers were forced to close (about thirty-three of them had already done so by 1925), the strongest, on the other hand, incorporated modern machinery and managed to increase their production. The Punta Alegre Sugar Company increased its output by 54 percent; the Cuban Dominican Company, by 65 percent; the General Sugar Company, by 135 percent; the Antilla Sugar Company, by 359 percent.

Despite the fact that the number of mills decreased (from about 200 to 157), production between 1922–1923 and 1925 rose considerably.

From then on the predominance of North American sugar interests was definitive. According to the Commission on Cuban Affairs' Report, which has been cited previously, in 1927, out of 175 active sugar mills, 71 were American; 14 were owned by mixed American and Cuban capital; 10 were Canadian or half Canadian and half Cuban; 15 belonged to Spaniards or Frenchmen; and 4 belonged to an Englishman who had been born in Cuba. The Report added that at that time there had been a great number of transfers of property and important mergers and that the situation had changed somewhat and that out of 160 active mills, 70 were definitively American. It pointed out that the most characteristic

[27] *Problems of the New Cuba,* p. 221. On pp. 230–232 the same process in relation to financing of production is described.

feature of the situation was the ownership and control by the banks of the sugar industry.

> Nine mills are controlled by the National City Bank, eight of them through the General Sugar Estates, Inc. The Royal Bank of Canada operates an even larger number of mills, most of them through the Sugar Plantations Operating Company. It has sought to preserve title for original owners in many cases, and has in other cases sought to reconstitute them under individual control, with occasional success. The Chase National Bank of New York, in addition to its interest in the new Atlantic & Gulf Company and in Punta Alegre, has three mills on its hands. Other bank-owned mills include Macareño, largely the property of the National Shawmut Bank of Boston; Caracas and Amazonas, belonging to the First National Bank of Boston; and Covadonga, in which the Canadian Bank of Commerce has a one-third interest.
>
> The American-owned mills in the strongest position financially are those owned outright by American refineries or by holding companies to which refineries belong. These include Cunagua and Jaronú, belonging to the American Sugar Refining Company; Preston and Boston, which belong to the United Fruit Company; and Chaparra, Delicias, Mercedita, Tinguaro, Unidad and Constancia (A), which are the property of the Cuban-American Sugar Company. Hershey, Rosario and San Antonio belong to the Hershey Corporation.[28]

The control of a large part of the Cuban sugar production, however, did not prevent North American interests from competing in sugar production in possessions under United States control (Hawaii, Puerto Rico, the Philippines). Production in these areas rose steadily as a result of the tariff of 1922 and contributed to heightening the depressive pressure on world sugar prices.

A summary of the evolution of the sugar industry during the period under consideration would allow one to reach the following conclusions.

The industry's development required not only favorable natural conditions but the incorporation of other resources lacking on the island. When these resources were combined in the necessary proportions, there followed a phase of growing specialization in sugar production for export. This process, at first glance, produced a notable increase in exports. The manner in which adjustments were made that led to the strong increase of sugar production and

[28] Ibid., pp. 226–228.

TABLE 3–10 PROPORTIONS OF AMERICAN SUGAR SUPPLIES

Years	Cuba	Continental USA	Island Areas (U.S.)
1912–1913	50.4	22.4	25.2
1914–1916	49.3	24.0	25.6
1917–1921	48.6	23.5	23.9
1922–1926	56.2	19.4	23.0
1927–1930	49.4	18.4	31.8
1931	37.4	23.6	38.6
1932	28.2	23.7	47.7
1933	25.3	26.6	47.9
1934	29.4	28.1	42.3

SOURCE: *Problems of the New Cuba*, p. 236.

export, the manner in which international markets were reached, the competition or obstacles that had to be overcome, and the response to changing market conditions are details which have been surveyed in the preceding pages. How did these characteristics of the development of the sugar industry operate upon the economy as a whole? This will be the subject of the following section.

Through the varying stages of its development the industry required changes in its structure and also in its degree of technological development in order to be able to compete in international markets under prevailing world trade conditions. The most important changes were concentration of production in a few centrales, which monopolized the colonos' cane supply, and modernization of the productive process, which eliminated numerous antiquated mills and, later on, financially weaker firms which were not in a position to make investments that might substantially reduce production costs during periods of declining prices.

Due to the nature of the industry, this meant that the more highly efficient the production and the more modern technology it incorporated, the more concentrated it became and, hence, the more capital-intensive in comparison to its organization prior to the centrales.

As for the effects that the income created by this industry might have produced in the economy as a whole, the following may be observed:

1. Since it was more capital-intensive and capital was an external, that is, *nonresident* factor, a substantial part of this income was transferred abroad.

2. Since labor was mostly unskilled and the bulk of cash salaries extremely low, the role of labor, a *resident* factor, was minor, and labor's share of the income was meager.

As for the input demands that the industry required (backward linkages),[29] they too were small for two reasons: (1) The enormous specialization of the Cuban economy (which even required the import of bags for marketing the sugar), and (2) the fact that the island's economy could not supply the demands for machinery and transportation needed in the initial development of sugar production. As for forward linkages, inasmuch as raw sugar was generally refined in the United States, the reduction in production costs benefited those engaged in the refining of the final product.

Thus, because of its technological features, the industry neither exhibits more than a few linkages nor favors a more diversified income distribution and thereby lacks significant multiplying effects on the demand side (Watkins's demand linkages).[30] This,

[29] The concept of linkage, the means by which the export activity generates demands in the domestic sector or provides it with lower cost imputs, was developed by Hirschman who differentiates: (a) backward linkages, those related with the demand to provide inputs and (b) forward linkages, that is, all activity which by its own nature provides final demand and induces the utilization of its products when they reduce their costs as inputs of new activities. Cf. A. Hirschman, *The Strategy of Economic Development* (New Haven, Conn.: Yale University Press, 1965), p. 100.

[30] Final demand linkage will tend to be higher, the higher the average level of income and the more equal its distribution. At a higher level of income, consumers are likely to be able to buy a range of goods and services which lend themselves to domestic production by advanced industrial techniques. Where the distribution is relatively unequal, the demand will be for subsistence goods and the lower end of the income scales and for luxuries at the upper end. The more equal the distribution the less the likelihood of opulent luxury importers and the greater the likelihood of a broadly based market for mass-produced goods.

Cf. Melville H. Watkins, "A Staple Theory of Economic Growth," *The Canadian Journal of Economics and Political Science,* vol. 29, no. 2 (May 1963), p. 146.

TABLE 3–11 CUBAN EXPORTS FOR SEVERAL YEARS
(*in thousands of tons*)

1919	575
1920	794
1925	354
1932	81

SOURCE: IBRD, *Report on Cuba,* p. 729.

as earlier noted, was accentuated by the seasonal nature of sugar production. The fact that the harvest lasted only four months of the year means that a larger number of workers lived in subsistent conditions the remainder of the year, the "dead season." This is reflected not only in broad seasonal fluctuations of prices, but in the incomes of a mass of people who received no cash salaries during that period. Of about 800,000 sugar employees, around 440,000 (55 percent) were temporary workers.

Extreme specialization plus the fact that the demand of the external market did not increase at the same rate is reflected in the extreme vulnerability of sugar exports, owing not only to the domestic incapacity to absorb the surplus but also to the inelasticity of the international demand for sugar. In Table 3–11 the extremely drastic decline of sugar exports after 1920 and especially after 1925 is observable, which gives some idea of the drastic fluctuation of demand.

Not only was international demand inelastic with respect to declining prices, but also sugar consumption in the traditional consumer countries (particularly the United States) was a decreasing function of their national income. Because of the high impact which exports had on the national income, these fluctuations were also reflected in income fluctuations, which was even more serious. This can be seen in Figure 3–2 taken from the report made on Cuba by the World Bank on fluctuations in exports and national income.

As may be observed, national income correlates closely with exports. In this case the drastic fluctuation of the latter has an

FIGURE 3–2 EXPORTS, IMPORTS, AND NATIONAL INCOME OF CUBA BETWEEN 1903 AND 1930

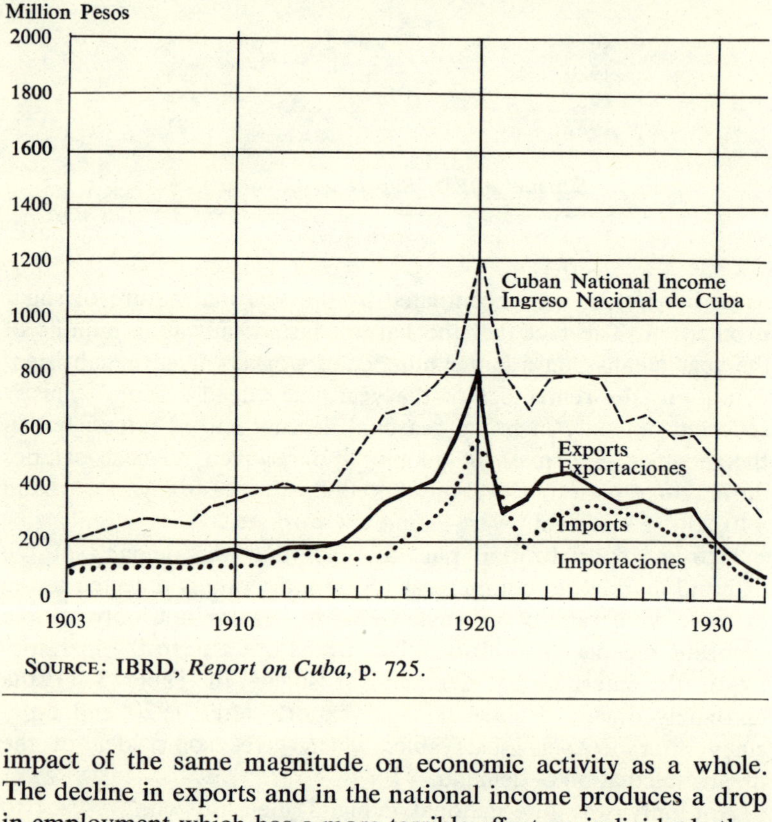

SOURCE: IBRD, *Report on Cuba,* p. 725.

impact of the same magnitude on economic activity as a whole. The decline in exports and in the national income produces a drop in employment which has a more terrible effect on individuals than mere statistics can reflect. It is noteworthy that these effects on society were foreseen a long time before by a lucid generation of Cuban intellectuals (among whom Ramiro Guerra and Fernando Ortiz were outstanding figures), as well as by observers and impartial investigators outside of Cuba itself. These problems assumed central importance in the revolutionary schemes formulated by Fidel Castro and his followers many years later.

4
CHILE: MINING EXPORTS

Unlike other regions, most notably the Río de la Plata, where the enormous distance between production zones and potential markets made commercial agriculture utterly impossible, Chile as early as the colonial period possessed a market in Peru and in Upper Peru (Bolivia) which was an outgrowth of the early division of labor imposed by the mining economy.[1]

Though independence brought with it freedom of trade, which facilitated the entry of European goods into Chile, there was no surge in exports.[2] In fact, for a time during the War for Independence the Peruvian market was closed to Chilean goods.[3] Silver

[1] Concerning agriculture during the colonial period, see Claudio Gay, *Historia física y política de Chile* (Paris: Fain and Thunot, 1844). References to trade with Peru in the colonial period are in Francisco Encina, *Nuestra inferioridad económica, sus causas y sus consecuencias* (Santiago: Editorial Universitaria, 1955), pp. 72–73. See also Luis Galdames, *Geografía económica de Chile* (Santiago: Imprenta Universitaria, 1911), p. 133. He calculates that trade during the seventeenth century was barely 12,000 fanegas of wheat per year.

[2] The decree of February 21, 1811, of the provisional government junta during the Patria Vieja permitted free entry rights through the ports of Valdivia, Valparaiso, and Coquinbo. This was formalized by the Free Trade Law (Reglamento de Libre Comercio) of 1813. The measure, however, was more limited than it would seem.

> Far from establishing a reign of free trade—as its title might erroneously suggest—this ruling established a customs tariff of 30 percent ad valorem on the introduction of foreign goods and products. The decision to lift this customs barrier stemmed from complex considerations induced as much by the need to collect funds for the public treasury as from the desire to encourage national industry and to avoid harm to industries in neighboring nations. Claudio Véliz, *Historia de la marina mercante de Chile* (Santiago: Ediciones de la Universidad de Chile, 1961), p. 22.

[3] Trade with Europe dated from the colonial period with permissions granting free shipping around Cape Horn. The independence movement

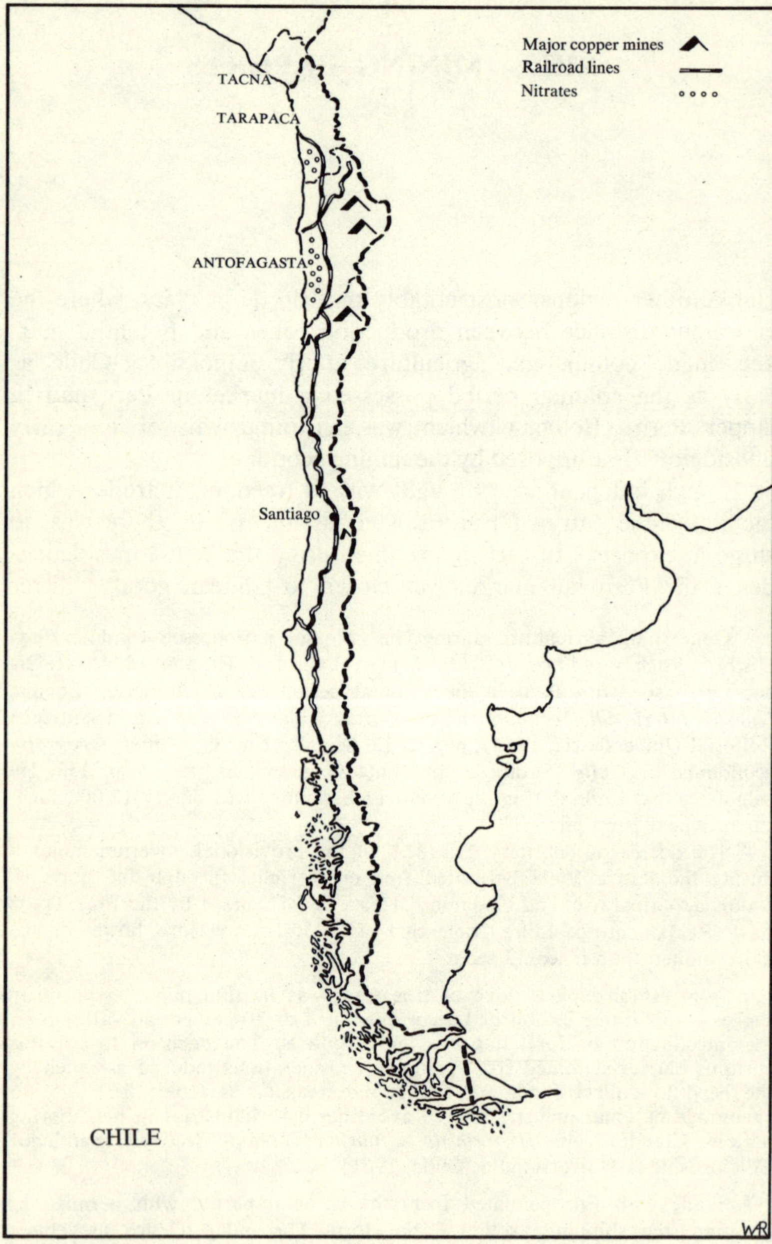

WILLOW ROBERTS

deposits were discovered in Chañarcillo in 1832, but it was actually after 1834 that silver and copper production showed an appreciable rise.[4]

According to Daniel Martner:

> During that year of 1834 economic activity became increasingly regularized, agriculture showed marked improvement, as did mining, bringing silver production to 164,935 marks an ounce per year with a value of $1,484,416, or seven-fold that of the colonial period, copper production amounted to 77,265 quintals with a value of $1,081,710, excluding from these figures 36,850 quintals of mineral copper with a value of $66,791—bringing it to a total of three times higher than that of the colonial period, while gold production rose to 3,852 marks an ounce with a value of $525,231. Almost all of this output was for export with the exception of gold which was minted domestically.[5]

The evolution of silver and copper production is shown in Tables 4–1 and 4–2.

Between 1840 and 1855 silver production multiplied sixfold. Copper production, which amounted to 6,500 tons in 1841–1843, climbed to 50,000 tons in the 1860s. At that time Chilean production represented 40 percent of the world supply of copper and 65

---

contributed to a steady increase in the entry of European products, and this influx provoked a grave commercial crisis. This is pointed out by Martner. Nevertheless, he upholds the thesis that independence resulted from the need to liberalize trade. He claims that the obstacles imposed by Spain on free trade were a hindrance to Chilean development. This thesis, which is fairly prevalent in the historiography of the struggles for independence, has been reiterated by Hernan Ramírez de Necochea, "Economic origins of Independence" in R. A. Humphreys and John Lynch, *The Origins of the Latin American Revolutions 1808–1826* (New York: Alfred A. Knopf, 1966), pp. 169–172. There is no evidence, however, that Chile, independence notwithstanding, would have increased her export activity at least until 1830.

[4] Pierre Denis, "Chili" in P. Vidal de la Blache, *Géographie Universelle,* vol. 15, p. 348, Amérique du Sud (2d part) (Paris: Librairie Armand Colin, 1927).

[5] Daniel Martner, *Estudio de la política comercial chilena en la historia económica nacional,* vol. I (Santiago: Imprenta Universitaria, 1923), p. 178. The figures with dollar signs are Chilean pesos.

TABLE 4–1 SILVER PRODUCTION, 1801–1855

Years	**Annual Production Average (in grams)**
1801–1810	7,000,000
1811–1820	10,000,000
1821–1830	20,000,000
1831–1840	33,000,000
1841–1843	33,333,333
1844	32,313,411
1845	40,748,763
1846	42,295,321
1847	42,718,290
1848	52,873,495
1849	72,255,023
1850	95,839,820
1851	100,028,217
1852	145,620,268
1853	116,117,990
1854	168,861,026
1855	212,996,180

SOURCE: *Estadística Minera de Chile en 1910* (Santiago: Sociedad Nacional Minería, 1911), pp. 39–40.

percent of the British supply. Moreover, between 1844 and 1860, wheat production quintupled.[6]

Despite the fact that writers on this subject assume the pattern of growth to have been steady, the statistics employed by them would indicate a significant decline in agricultural output during the first two decades of the independence period.[7] This decline was directly related to a drop in the trade with Peru, hurt by Peruvian restrictions on Chilean imports. The rise in Chilean agricultural output during the middle decades of the nineteenth century can be attributed primarily to recovery of the Peruvian market, particularly after the Peruvian decree of 1840 which, in

[6] Aníbal Pinto Santa Cruz, *Chile, un caso de desarrollo frustrado* (Santiago: Editorial Universitaria S.A., 1962), p. 15.

[7] See ibid., p. 16.

TABLE 4–2 COPPER PRODUCTION, 1801–1870

Years	Annual Production Average (in kilograms)
1801–1820	1,500,000
1821–1835	2,044,000
1836–1843	6,454,000
1844	9,586,549
1845	8,542,398
1846	10,337,905
1847	9,768,887
1848	10,106,223
1849	10,647,399
1850	12,344,623
1851	8,370,739
1852	16,352,114
1853	15,017,291
1854	17,383,384
1855	21,846,720
1856	23,605,962
1857	25,467,852
1858	24,766,051
1859	23,388,678
1860	34,122,747
1861	33,616,812
1862	37,158,441
1863	31,733,712
1864	42,693,701
1865	41,211,211
1866	33,092,283
1867	43,167,441
1868	42,122,228
1869	51,802,487
1870	44,202,517

SOURCE: *Estadística Minera de Chile en 1910,* p. 42.

accordance with a Chilean request, lowered the tariff on Chilean wheat.[8]

[8] According to a provision in 1836, Chilean wheat paid 2 pesos per fanega, and 2 reales in excise tax per fanega of 135 kilos; this was reduced to 1 peso, 2 reales. Flour, which formerly paid 5 pesos, 32.3 reales per sack,

In 1841 the agricultural production was estimated at 40 million pesos.[9] From then on and all during Bulnes's presidency, there was a significant economic resurgence. The expansion of trade went hand in hand with the expansion of the merchant marine. Coastal trade had been placed in the hands of nationals as early as 1813 with the beginnings of independence—la Patria Vieja. This policy was reiterated during Prieto's presidency, which began on October 22, 1835, and resulted in a substantial increase in the national fleet.[10] Later the railway network was added which transported the production of the central agricultural zone to the coast.[11]

There was one particular event which produced a significant change in the direction of foreign trade and provided a tremendous impetus to agricultural exports: the California gold rush of 1848, which attracted a heavy influx of people to those previously deserted lands.[12] Since they went to California not to cultivate land, but to search for gold and since land transportation was extremely costly in the United States prior to the opening of the Panama Canal (though the California market provided an important stimulus for the Canal project), Chile found itself in an

---

would henceforth pay the government only 2 pesos, 4 reales and 4 reales in excise taxes per quintal. Martner, *Estudio de la política comercial chilena,* p. 166.

[9] One Chilean peso was equivalent to 45 English pence or 45d. The "d" is the abbreviation of pence. The equivalence in pence is employed because of the modification of the value of Chilean currency.

[10] See Véliz, *Historia de la marina mercante,* chap. 1. In 1852 there were 215 sailboats with a tonnage of 41,500 tons, in 1866 this rose to 247 sailboats of 66,011 tons, and 11 steamboats with 2,207 tons. In 1866 the provision favoring nationals was repealed, and in 1868 there were only 19 sailboats with a tonnage of 2,780 tons, and two steamships with 644 tons; the rest were foreign vessels. Martner, *Estudio de la política comercial chilena,* p. 150.

[11] In 1849 a concession was granted to the English engineer William Wheelwright. Work on the line, Santiago-Valparaíso, which began in 1852, ended eleven years later in 1863 with only 187 kilometers of track having been built. Ibid., p. 241.

[12] Galdames, *Geografía económica de Chile,* p. 141, also notes the importance of the construction of the first national railroads, the establishment of the National Society of Agriculture, and the abolition of the right of primogeniture and of the tithe.

excellent position to supply the new demand. Production received strong incentives from the sharp price rise which occurred in the gold rush territory. Exports, which in 1844 amounted to 6.1 million pesos rose rapidly in 1848 and in the two subsequent years, and by 1850 they reached 12.4 million pesos.[13] During the Manuel Montt administration, economic activity, especially railroads, received hearty encouragement. Exports doubled in the space of a decade: in 1860 they reached 25 million pesos. But disquieting circumstances then emerged. Projects for the Panama Canal threatened agricultural production with the loss of the heretofore avid Californian market. In the field of mineral production a drop in copper prices (in 1860 copper represented 56 percent of the total Chilean exports) was an important blow to foreign trade.

In 1861, the inaugural year of the Pérez administration, Chilean exports fell 20 percent. This was due not only to the price drop, but to the fall in production in Chañarcillo.

Sepúlveda, one of the best-informed writers on this subject, says that Chile's agrarian production was intended for the European market, and he belittles the importance of the California and Australia markets.[14] If that were the case, two distinct circumstances blocked any definitive agricultural expansion: the declining price trend in world trade dating from 1873 and, perhaps more important, the growing competition from Argentine production. Since Argentina was better located with respect to Europe and had better land, it was able to displace Chile not only in its own domestic market, but also, finally and conclusively, from the European market.[15]

Exports, which in 1860 amounted to 25 million pesos (43 3/4d), in 1870 came only to 27 million pesos (45 5/8d), a relatively slow growth. Imports, on the other hand, rose in a larger proportion, producing an unfavorable balance of trade for the first time in 1870 (imports totaled 28.2 million pesos; exports, 27.0 million). After 1870 and until 1875 exports climbed because of

[13] Martner, *Estudio de la política comercial chilena,* p. 224.

[14] Sepúlveda, *El Trigo Chileno en el mercado mundial,* cited by Pinto, *Chile,* p. 28.

[15] Francisco Encina, *Nuestra inferioridad económica,* p. 84.

the discoveries in 1870 of copper deposits in Caracoles and nitrate in Antofagasta.[16]

In 1875 exports rose to 35 million pesos (43 13/16d) but, nonetheless, were exceeded by imports (38.1 million). After 1876 poor harvests and a decline in prices as well as in copper production were reflected in a strong drop (16 percent) in exports, from 37.8 million pesos in 1876 to 31.7 million pesos in 1878.[17] This drop led to a serious crisis in the balance of payments and to the decision in 1878 to impose monetary inconvertibility, which was decreed for the first time in a country characterized since 1830 not only for its political stability, but also for its monetary stability. Inconvertibility, as could be expected, was translated into a steady devaluation of Chilean currency.[18]

From 1876–1878 (the Pinto administration) foreign trade declined substantially, from 37.8 million pesos in 1876 to 29.7 million pesos in 1877 to 31.7 million pesos in 1878, constituting, as previously mentioned, an important cause of the crisis of 1878. But in the following years, because of production in the great new nitrate mines of the north, conditions improved, and in 1880 exports amounted to 51.7 million pesos, a rise of 64.5 percent in two years. The end of the War of the Pacific (1879–1884), which led to the definitive incorporation of the provinces of Antofagasta and Tarapacá with their nitrate deposits, brought a strong and steady rise in exports. In 1881 nitrate exports reached 400,000 tons (a 45 percent increase over the previous year).

Meanwhile the value of imports amounted to only 39.4 million

[16] Galdames, *Geografía económica de Chile,* p. 99; Martner, *Estudio de la política comercial chilena,* p. 301. Although most of the nitrate mines of Antofagasta and Tarapacá did not belong to Chile, Chilean capital and labor had been invested in them. The measures adapted by Peru and Bolivia with regard to Chilean companies provided some of the causes for the subsequent war. With respect to this, see Oscar Bermúdez, *Historia del salitre desde sus orígenes hasta la guerra del Pacífico* (Santiago: Ediciones de la Universidad de Chile, 1963), pp. 366 et seq.

[17] Denis, "Chili," p. 348.

[18] With respect to this see Frank W. Fetter, *Monetary Inflation in Chile* (Princeton, N.J.: Princeton University Press, 1931). Fetter maintains that it was not the negative balances in the balance of payments which led to inconvertibility and devaluation, but the need of the indebted classes to liquidate their debts at a lower cost.

TABLE 4–3 EXCHANGE RATE OF THE CHILEAN PESO IN TERMS OF ENGLISH PENCE FROM 1830 TO 1910

Year	Average	Year	Average
1830	44	1870	$45\frac{5}{8}$
1831	$44\frac{1}{2}$	1871	$45\frac{15}{16}$
1832	45	1872	$46\frac{3}{8}$
1833	$44\frac{5}{8}$	1873	$44\frac{13}{16}$
1834	$45\frac{3}{4}$	1874	$44\frac{5}{8}$
1835	$44\frac{3}{4}$	1875	$43\frac{13}{16}$
1836	$44\frac{3}{4}$	1876	$40\frac{9}{16}$
1837	$44\frac{11}{16}$	1877	$42\frac{1}{16}$
1838	45	1878	$39\frac{5}{8}$
1839	$45\frac{1}{2}$	1879	33
1840	$45\frac{1}{4}$	1880	$30\frac{7}{8}$
1841	$45\frac{1}{2}$	1881	$30\frac{15}{16}$
1842	$45\frac{3}{4}$	1882	$35\frac{3}{8}$
1843	$45\frac{1}{2}$	1883	$35\frac{1}{4}$
1844	$44\frac{11}{16}$	1884	$31\frac{3}{4}$
1845	$44\frac{1}{2}$	1885	$25\frac{7}{16}$
1846	$44\frac{7}{16}$	1886	$23\frac{15}{16}$
1847	44	1887	$24\frac{1}{2}$
1848	$43\frac{3}{8}$	1888	$26\frac{1}{4}$
1849	$44\frac{15}{16}$	1889	$26\frac{9}{16}$
1850	$46\frac{3}{16}$	1890	$24\frac{1}{16}$
1851	$45\frac{13}{16}$	1891	$18\frac{13}{16}$
1852	46	1892	$18\frac{13}{16}$
1853	$47\frac{1}{4}$	1893	15
1854	45	1894	$12\frac{9}{16}$
1855	$45\frac{3}{4}$	1895	$16\frac{13}{16}$
1856	$45\frac{5}{8}$	1896	$17\frac{7}{16}$
1857	$45\frac{3}{4}$	1897	$17\frac{9}{16}$
1858	$45\frac{5}{16}$	1898	$15\frac{11}{16}$
1859	$45\frac{5}{8}$	1899	$14\frac{1}{2}$
1860	$43\frac{3}{4}$	1900	$16\frac{4}{5}$
1861	$44\frac{11}{16}$	1901	$16\frac{1}{8}$
1862	$45\frac{7}{16}$	1902	$15\frac{1}{4}$
1863	$43\frac{7}{8}$	1903	$16\frac{3}{5}$
1864	$44\frac{5}{16}$	1904	$16\frac{4}{9}$
1865	$45\frac{13}{16}$	1905	$15\frac{3}{4}$
1866	$46\frac{9}{16}$	1906	$14\frac{11}{16}$
1867	$46\frac{13}{16}$	1907	$11\frac{15}{16}$
1868	$46\frac{1}{16}$	1908	$9\frac{17}{32}$
1869	$46\frac{1}{16}$	1909	$10\frac{25}{31}$
		1910	$10\frac{57}{64}$

SOURCE: *Estadística Minera de Chile en 1910*, p. 101.

TABLE 4–4 EXPORTS OF CHILEAN NITRATE, 1879–1932

Years	Nitrate (tons)	Years	Nitrate (tons)
1879	125,000	1906	1,761,300
1880	275,000	1907	1,882,900
1881	400,000	1908	1,849,800
1882	490,000	1909	2,328,700
1883	580,000	1910	2,357,200
1884	510,000	1911	2,495,700
1885	450,000	1912	2,690,600
1886	525,000	1913	2,702,600
1887	750,000	1914	1,475,300
1888	800,000	1915	2,543,200
1889	920,000	1916	2,863,500
1890	1,000,000	1917	2,913,000
1891	800,000	1918	1,794,300
1892	900,000	1919	2,207,000
1893	1,025,000	1920	2,051,500
1894	1,200,000	1921	613,600
1895	1,250,000	1922	2,106,100
1896	1,200,000	1923	2,175,600
1897	1,300,000	1924	2,565,900
1898	1,350,000	1925	2,249,000
1899	1,425,000	1926	1,545,400
1900	1,476,000	1927	2,872,400
1901	1,298,000	1928	2,960,900
1902	1,338,900	1929	2,199,100
1903	1,486,400	1930	1,681,800
1904	1,613,900	1931	920,100
1905	1,669,400	1932	269,800

SOURCE: Dirección General de Estadística, *Sinopsis Geográfico. Estadística de la República de Chile* (Santiago: n.p., 1933), pp. 199–200.

pesos; this difference permitted the solution of the balance of payments deficit which was the origin of the crisis of 1878. Although the nitrate boom provided a new and powerful export activity when others were declining, it also resulted in a particular specialization in exports, which, until then, had been more diversified. In effect, agriculture and mining had oscillated in different but more or less even proportions in the total value of exports: agriculture

TABLE 4–5 CHILEAN EXPORTS
INCLUDING GOLD AND COPPER
(*in millions of gold pesos of 18d*)

Year	**Chilean Exports**
1900	167.7
1910	328.8
1920	778.9

SOURCE: Summary from Chilean Public Treasury from 1883 to 1914, quoted by Pinto, *Chile,* p. 103.

reached 45 percent of total exports in 1845–1850, and within mining activities there existed various categories—silver, copper, and gold. Following the strong surge in nitrate output in 1881, mining grew to represent 78 percent of Chilean exports, and agriculture, merely 16.5 percent, with other items accounting for 5 percent. Nitrate exports were ahead of all others with 25.9 million pesos and were followed by copper with 16.3 million while wheat and flour amounted to 5.5 million pesos.[19]

While copper exports underwent a severe crisis due to high production costs among Chilean firms, nitrates, at least until 1920, provided Chile with a steadily rising export activity.

During this period there was a strong impetus toward economic development in railroad construction, other forms of transportation, and infrastructure works. Although these projects to modernize the infrastructure of production began during the administration of Manuel Montt (1850–1860), they attained significant proportions during José Manuel Balmaceda's presidency (1886–1891), when the government intervened in the economy in order to promote progress. The portion of government budgetary expenses devoted to economic development increased notably during Balmaceda's presidency and continued in varying degrees during subsequent administrations, thus indicating a significant modernization of the Chilean government. Later on, when the nitrate deposits located in territories occupied during the war passed into

19 Martner, *Estudio de la política comercial chilena,* p. 365.

the hands of the Chilean government, the latter, influenced by the liberal ideas spread by Courcelle Seneueil, gave up its role in the exploitation of nitrate and turned it over to private hands.[20] Because the government was convinced that nitrate would be better managed by private capital and, further, that the government would receive greater profits from taxes than from direct exploitation, a process of rapid denationalization was started during Jorge Montt's presidency (1891–1901). Participation by foreign interests in this exploitation resulted not only from a net investment of capital (estimates of which are lacking), but also from a process of reclaiming bonds held by creditors against the Peruvian government and that were totally devaluated in the market.[21] Most of the foreign capital in the nitrate industry came from the United Kingdom. At that time the importance of North American capital was limited. On the other hand, Chilean investments in nitrate decreased between 1884 and 1901, while the opposite occurred with British investments.

Differing estimates exist on the profits yielded by nitrates. According to Martner's calculations, prior to 1920 they amounted to 5.754 million pesos (18d), of which he believed that at least 50 percent had remained in the country as payment for domestic production factors and taxes. Carlos Vicuña's estimate is shown in Table 4–6.

Since nitrate demands a much less complicated technology than was subsequently utilized for copper, its requirements (in labor

[20] On the investment activities of the government, see Judson M. De Cew, *The Chilean Budget: 1833–1914* (New Haven, Conn.: 1969, manuscript). Initially, the nitrate mines were under military occupation; the government supervised their development and granted sales concession for a 2.5 percent commission. Cf. Francisco Encina, *Historia de Chile* (Santiago: Ed. Nacimiento, 1955).

[21] The bonds and certificates transferred by the Peruvian government as payment for the plants, which had lost almost all value, suddenly began to be sought by "mysterious purchasers who paid ten and even twenty percent of their nominal value for them, in despised *soles*." When the Chilean government's decision went into effect, the new holders became the owners of the most valuable part of the industry. A central figure in this absurd as well as suspicious drama was the legendary case of Mr. John T. North who, irony of ironies, contrived a fantastic speculation which transformed him into the "nitrate king," all with Chilean capital provided by the Bank of Valparaiso. Pinto, *Chile,* p. 55.

TABLE 4–6 DISTRIBUTION OF EARNINGS FROM NITRATE
(*in millions of pounds and percentages*)

	Millions of Pounds	**Percentages**
Profits	500	58.8
Fiscal Earnings	250	29.4
Labor	100	11.8
Total	850	100

SOURCE: Carlos Vicuña quoted by Pinto, *Chile,* p. 56.

and other inputs of production) could be supplied within the country. Aside from the considerable proportion of profits paid to nonresident factors, a share of the income generated by this activity undoubtedly remained within the country in payment for the inputs of production and in other forms such as commercialization costs, transportation, construction, warehouses, dwellings, and so forth. In addition, other payments were made abroad for commercialization, maritime transport, freight, and insurance which do not appear in Vicuña's estimates to be able to determine, even in a very general way, the proportion of income produced by the exploitation of nitrates that remained in Chile. It is obvious that the part that corresponded to government taxes and labor remained in Chile.

COPPER: HIGH TECHNOLOGY MINING

Because Chile lacked the technological knowledge which would have permitted the exploitation of mines to greater depths in search of new veins, the mines which had existed since the 1830s were depleted by 1880. Chile then lost its position as the most efficient, low-cost copper producer, as Table 4–7 indicates.

At the time of the War of the Pacific copper deposits were discovered in the western part of the United States, which meant that Chile's hitherto privileged position in copper production was usurped. As Clark Reynolds says, "By the turn of the century, Chilean copper mining was diversified with small deposits being

TABLE 4–7 WORLD PRODUCTION OF COPPER AND CHILEAN PARTICIPATION

Years	World Copper Production (in metric tons)	Percentage of Chilean Copper
1880	156,422	25.30
1881	165,983	24.07
1882	184,528	24.44
1883	202,596	19.57
1884	223,773	19.92
1885	229,201	17.37
1886	220,559	17.15
1887	227,379	13.1
1888	262,154	19.03
1889	265,384	9.39
1890	273,766	9.73
1891	283,861	7.35
1892	315,440	6.74
1893	308,386	7.52
1894	329,697	7.06
1895	339,918	6.59
1896	379,337	6.63
1897	406,126	5.20
1898	436,500	6.03
1899	479,800	5.36
1900	493,861	5.61
1901	524,894	5.74
1902	549,956	4.92
1903	574,873	5.20
1904	640,935	4.84
1905	708,810	4.11

SOURCE: *Estadística Minera de Chile en 1910*, p. 76.

worked up and down the land—no one producing more than 20,000 tons of ore annually. Methods were generally still very crude and few mines employed technically trained personnel."[22]

Copper activity began to languish, overwhelmed by the combination of declining prices and rising costs.

[22] Clark Reynolds, "Development Problems of an Export Economy," in Markos Mamalakis and Clark Reynolds, *Essays on the Chilean Economy* (Homewood, Ill.: Richard Irwin, 1965), p. 213.

TABLE 4–8 THE PRICES OF BAR COPPER IN ENGLAND

Year	Average Annual Price per English Ton, 1,016 Kilograms		
	£	*s*	*d*
1880	62	14	7
1881	61	16	9
1882	66	10	5
1883	62	17	11
1884	53	17	6
1885	43	11	0
1886	40	1	8
1887	46	0	5
1888	81	11	3
1889	49	14	8
1890	54	5	3
1891	51	9	4
1892	45	13	2
1893	43	15	6
1894	40	7	4

SOURCE: *Estadística Minera de Chile en 1910*, p. 76.

On the other hand, during the first decade of the twentieth century, a profound technological revolution took place in the copper industry which required vertical integration, the use of highly capital-intensive techniques, concentration, and the incorporation of the smelting process. The change in the structure of the industry, which was to return Chile to its number one position in copper export, also meant a change in the control of the property of the copper mines and its concentration in the hands of three large North American companies.

According to Pierre Denis:

> After 1875, production once more declined, but after 1915 it suddenly rose again, with the founding of great metallurgical firms which employed low-grade minerals. Among the three Chilean firms of this type, two were situated in desert regions: Chuquicamata, near Calama (22° latitude South) and Potrerillos, 110 kilometers east of Chañaral (26°30′). These are powerful companies, with North American capital, capable of processing 10,000 tons of minerals a

day, through electrolysis and converters, and provided with coastal installations for shipping the metal, as well as electrothermal factories with high tension lines to conduct current to the mines. Secondary mines and small foundries at the ports are intermittently active.[23]

In fact, the transformation and expansion process began in 1904 with Braden Copper's exploitation of El Teniente mine near Santiago. It continued with Chuquicamata on the Andean slope and with Potrerillos, exploited at first by British capital and transferred subsequently to Guggenheim. The growth of copper production was slow at first. In 1900 the value of its output was insignificant; in 1913 it amounted to 2.6 million pounds in comparison to nitrate's 23.9 million pounds; in 1924 it reached 45 million dollars (about 14 million pounds). At that point the organization of the industry was based on the ABC companies, the "three greats." Company A was Andes Copper; B was Braden; and C was Chile Exploration Company-Chuquicamata. Companies A and C belonged to Anaconda Copper, and B belonged to Kennecott Copper Company.

Copper production rose at a very high rate after World War I. From 1925 to 1959 its cumulative rate of growth was 3.9 percent annually, which is quite different from the rates of growth of the Chilean economy as a whole for that same period. Reynolds calculates that the economy grew at an annual rate of growth of 1 percent per capita, a considerably less successful figure.[24] As late as 1956 the role of copper in the Chilean economy was decisive. It represented 11 percent of the Gross Domestic Product (GDP), 50 percent of exports, and 20 percent of government revenue.[25] Nevertheless, it is immediately apparent that the copper industry's rate of growth was not matched by that of the country as a whole. To what was this due?

First of all, copper constituted for a considerable period of time a typical foreign enclave. In 1920 Chilean participation in copper sales amounted to only 11 percent.[26] At the same time Chilean

[23] Denis, "Chili," p. 348.

[24] Reynolds, "Development Problems," p. 279.

[25] Ibid., pp. 259, 319.

[26] Ibid., p. 219. Reynolds cites Macchiavello Varas, *El problema de la industria del cobre en Chile y sus proyecciones económicas y sociales* (Santiago, 1923), p. 108.

TABLE 4–9 CHILEAN PARTICIPATION IN THE EARNINGS OF VARIOUS MINING INDUSTRIES IN 1920

Minerals	Percentage of Chilean Participation in the Earnings of Mining Production
Copper	11
Nitrate	56
Gold	35
Silver	38
Coal	91

SOURCE: Reynolds, "Development Problems," p. 219.

participation in the production of nitrate, coal, gold, and silver was much more important.

The peculiar circumstances in the copper industry were the result of several factors:

1. The fact that the companies were controlled by foreign capital, and, hence, their profits were sent abroad.

2. The copper industry was highly capital-intensive so that the proportion of labor employed (despite relatively high per capita salaries) was lower. This, in fact, is its distinguishing characteristic. In 1920 the employees of the Gran Minería represented 0.5 percent of the Chilean population and no more than 1 percent of the labor force.[27] On the other hand, nitrates required a higher proportion of personnel distributed in a larger number of small firms (53,000 workers in 137 locations; adding other employees brings the total to 80,000). As for copper, in 1920 two companies employed 33,210 workers.

3. The fact that the industry required machinery of a complex technological nature prevented its being provided from within the country itself. The total amount of capital input, stock, and replacements were imported.

4. Finally, there is an additional reason to explain the low local participation in the income derived from copper. The copper industry, unlike nitrate, was exempt until 1925 from all taxes. Only in 1925, when the income tax was imposed, did the copper industry

[27] Reynolds, "Development Problems," p. 223.

TABLE 4–10 NORTH AMERICAN AND CHILEAN FIRMS
(*percentages of total copper production*)

	1918	1920
North American Firms (2 companies)	87	80
Chilean Firms (more than 100 companies)	4	11

SOURCE: Reynolds, "Development Problems," p. 221.

begin to pay 4 percent of its profits in taxes. This exceptional and complete exemption was not maintained indefinitely, however. The laissez faire phase lasted until Arturo Alessandri's government (1920–1924), at which point the income tax was introduced for the first time. And after 1925 government participation in the earnings of the largest copper mines (Gran Minería) rose and reached its peak between 1950 and 1955.

According to Reynolds, the development of the Gran Minería can be classified into the following periods:[28]

1. Laissez faire (1904–1925). The industry, requiring the incorporation of modern technology and high investments, was transferred into foreign (North American) possession so that foreign firms controlled 80 percent of the country's production. Labor's participation was extremely low because of the scarce utilization of manpower in a highly capital-intensive operation. There was no input supply from the domestic sector since mining required highly specialized machinery that could only be obtained through importation. Nevertheless, copper activity was tax exempt.

Total copper sales of the three principal companies increased from 1.5 million dollars in 1912 to 50.1 million dollars in 1925. The portion of copper revenue that remained in the country seems small, 11 percent in 1920, according to Macchiavello Varas's figures.

2. Income Tax on Gran Minería (1925–1931). Despite the imposition of the income tax, the Chilean share of copper earnings continued to be modest. The Kemmerer Law established an addi-

[28] Mamalakis and Reynolds, *Essays on the Chilean Economy*, pp. 363, 219, 228.

tional payment of a 6 percent tax on the income of mines that was added to the 6 percent mining tax. While copper production rose from 45.8 to 50.1 million dollars between 1924 and 1925, direct assessment increased from 1.8 to 2.4 million dollars. During the Great Depression not only did mining production decline, so did the Chilean portion of its income:

TABLE 4–11 TOTAL CHILEAN EXPORTS AND COPPER PRODUCTION AND CHILEAN SHARE OF COPPER EARNINGS
(*in millions of dollars*)

	Chilean Exports	Copper Production[a]	Chilean Share of Copper Earnings
1929	277.4	110.8	33.2
1931	99.8	32.8	15.0
1932	34.1	11.3	6.7

[a] *A new tax that the United States imposed on copper imports of 4 cents per pound contributed to the drop in copper exports.*

SOURCE: Mamalakis and Reynolds, *Essays on the Chilean Economy,* pp. 375 and 377, and José Cademartori, *La Economía Chilena* (Santiago: Editorial Universitario, 1968), p. 214.

Chilean share of copper earnings or, as Reynolds terms it, "returned value,"[29] evolves in the following manner:

1920	11 percent
1925–1931	39 percent
1932–1937	37 percent
1937	28 percent

3. Foreign Exchange Control (1932–1937). In order to obtain a greater share of copper earnings, the Chilean government raised taxes on copper. It then established in general terms a new system

[29] We adhere here to Reynolds's study which defines "returned gross value" as the sum of all of the payments made by the export industry to domestic factors of production in the current or capital accounts. Reynolds, "Development Problems," pp. 219, 234, 275.

of control over the rate of exchange that was designed first of all to obtain foreign exchange in order to pay the foreign debt. It imposed a new tax on industry, whereby the latter was obliged to sell to the government the exchange obtained from any sales made at a price below the going market level. Since the real value of the Chilean peso followed a steady devaluation while the legal one remained stable, this difference became larger. But, despite all efforts, the Chilean share in earnings generated from copper exports remained low. It did not approach precrisis levels until 1937 (at which point it reached 25 million dollars).

4. Price Control (1938–1949). This period was characterized by different circumstances. The Frente-Popular (1938–1942), a center-left coalition (Radicals, Socialists, and Communists) came to power with a program emphasizing state intervention in the economy and attempting to impose restrictions on the powerful foreign companies.

The earthquake of 1939, which demanded an immediate response to the tremendous problems incurred by the destruction it brought, provided the government with its first instrument, CORFO —*La Corporación de Fomento Industrial* (Corporation for Industrial Development)—which obtained funds from an additional levy on the copper industry and from foreign loans. CORFO based its program on promoting Chilean industrialization so as to avoid the country's continued dependence on external phenomena, which it in no way controlled or determined but which affected it strongly.

In 1942 the government imposed an additional tax upon the extraordinary copper profits. Gran Minería at that point was selling dollars to the government for 19.37 pesos when the market value was 31.63 pesos. For the same reasons, investments during that period, as in the previous one, were minimal. The returned value, according to Reynolds's figures, was 36 percent in 1938, 58 percent in 1944, and 63 percent in 1949, with an average of 52 percent for the entire period compared with 37 percent for the previous period and 39 percent for the first.

During the war, a maximum price for copper was also established by the United States government. The response of the Chilean economy to increased participation in the copper industry was not, however, very encouraging. While the returned value in the Gross Domestic Product rose from 3.8 percent in 1938 to 5.7 percent in

1945, the growth rate of the GDP (1938–1945) was 4.1 yearly cumulative rate. The economy as a whole did not maintain the same rate as the export sector did.[30]

5. Government Intervention in Copper Marketing. Although the periods which follow fall outside the objectives of this study, it may be mentioned that the returned value rose in the following period from 1950 to 1955, insofar as prices rose because of the Korean War, reaching its peak of 72 percent.

6. New Deal Copper Law. To a certain extent the problems affecting the foreign sector, the need for foreign exchange, and the need to encourage exports led the government to a change in attitude concerning the industry which led to a reduction in the share that the government received through different taxes.

In the period between 1956 and 1959 the returned value decreased to 56 percent. If we apply Reynolds's concept as an indicator of *linkages* between export activity and the economy as a whole, we may conclude that it was primarily through the levying of taxes rather than payment to domestic factors (although these did increase after 1930 and World War II) that profits generated by a sector of the economy were transmitted to the rest of it. Although this might indicate that mining activity would not continue as an enclave, its effect was not impressive. Thus, while copper production between 1925 and 1959 climbed at an annual rate of 3.9 percent, the GNP rose at a much slower rate of 1 percent per capita. Had the returned value been invested, the growth of the Gross National Product would have attained a much higher rate.

Attempts at industrialization in the consumer sector, the social and subsidy policies, plus many additional factors such as inflation rising from a continual pressure of conflicting social sectors, all in varying degrees influenced this complex situation, which cannot be solely attributed to the way the economy was administered. To delve into these considerations, however, would require extending the scope of this study much more than its original objective.

30 Ibid., p. 243.

5

MODERNIZATION AND FOREIGN CAPITAL IN MEXICO, 1870–1910: THE PORFIRIO DÍAZ ERA

Porfirio Díaz took over the government of Mexico in 1876 and did not abandon it until 1911, except for the four-year nominal presidency of González (1880–1884). When he took power, the country was still isolated and backward, a condition which the government, imbued with ideas of modernization and progress, was determined to correct.

Mexico was predominantly an agrarian nation, in which the lack of transportation, internal customs duties on interstate commerce, and numerous fiscal and legal barriers presented serious obstacles to its efforts to establish a national market. The structure of land tenure, which consisted largely of huge self-sufficient entities known as *haciendas,* many of them owned by the church, plus lands owned by Indian communities—sparse, isolated, and self-sufficient—presented serious obstacles not merely in establishing a market on a national scale, but in linking one region with another or in placing the nation on a sound footing. Díaz was not the first to confront these problems with a program of modernization and national consolidation. Liberal and nationalist principles had already been established in the Constitution of 1857. That constitution provided for the abolition of interstate customs duties (*alcabala*), slavery, and forced labor debt peonage. These principles coincided with humanist ideas current among the liberal generation and simultaneously provided a potential labor supply for capitalist development. The liberal policies attempted to fulfill two basic objectives:

1. To put an end to the isolation of numerous local markets through the formation of a national market. This measure required the elimination of legal obstacles (interstate customs duties) as well as the establishment of a modern (less expensive) transportation system.

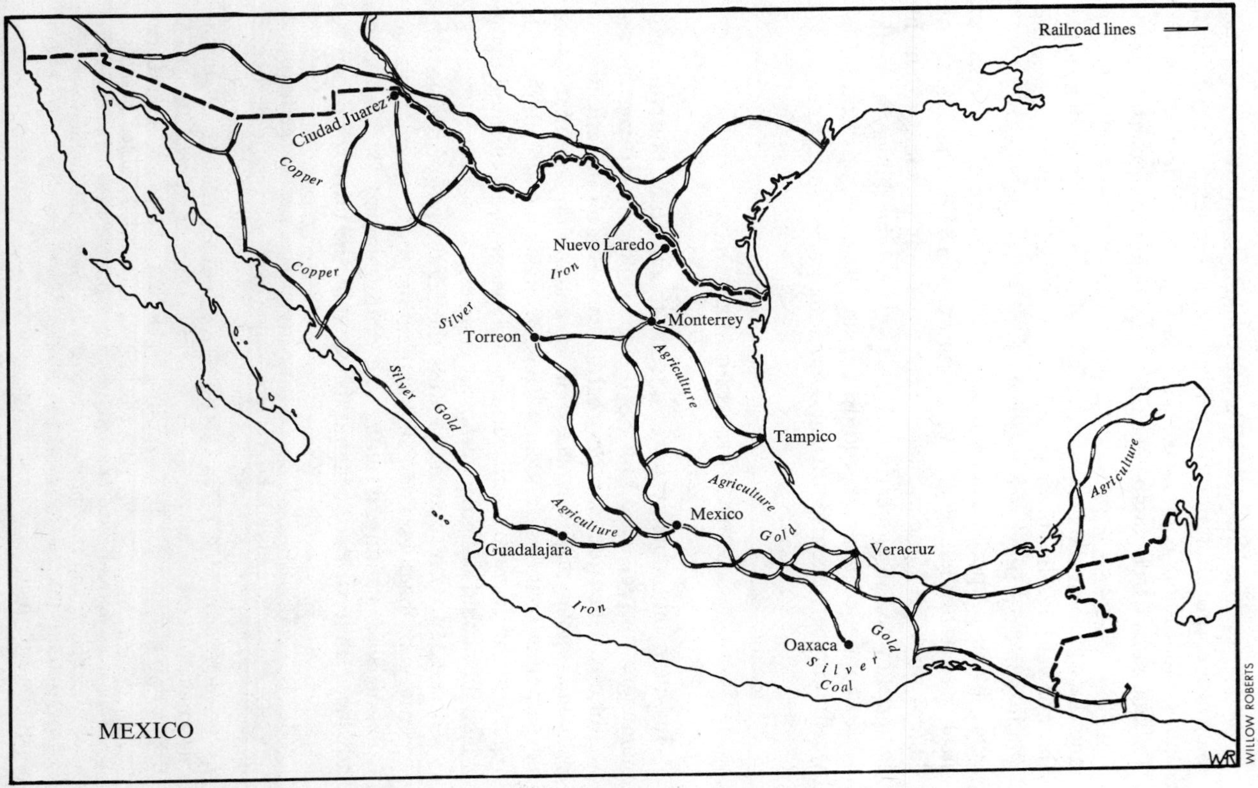
MEXICO
Railroad lines
Ciudad Juarez
Copper
Copper
Nuevo Laredo
Iron
Silver
Torreon
Monterrey
Agriculture
Silver
Gold
Tampico
Agriculture
Agriculture
Mexico
Gold
Guadalajara
Veracruz
Agriculture
Iron
Oaxaca
Gold
Silver
Coal
WR
WILLOW ROBERTS

2. To modify the country's landholding system through the partial incorporation into the market of unproductive church lands and small Indian communes. This last had the effect of forcing Indians into a free manpower pool, an equally indispensable prerequisite for the modernization program.[1] The French intervention and the war, plus the fact that the federal government under Juárez did not yet have the power it subsequently had to impose over the whole country, prevented realization of those policies except in some isolated aspects. This was reflected in the federal organization itself as established by the Constitution of 1857. The impact of liberal principles under Juárez was significant to some extent in land policy and in pioneering efforts to extend the railway network, which continued under Lerdo de Tejada.[2] The definitive push forward, however, occurred during Díaz's long administration.

Mexico under Porfirio Díaz

It would undoubtedly be erroneous to maintain that the economic growth registered in Mexico from 1880 to 1910 was the result of any deliberate plan or program based on an initially defined economic policy. Nevertheless, it is unquestionable that those participating in the processes of decision making, particularly with regard to the economy, had certain fairly clear goals in mind upon which they could design government policies.

These goals corresponded to ideas then dominant of terminating a century of backwardness by extricating the country from its isolation and guiding it along the path pursued by the more advanced nations. Public figures, infected by the fever for progress,

[1] Concerning church holdings arising from the sale of ecclesiastical property in conformance with deamortization laws of reform legislation during Juárez's first presidential term see Jean Bazant, *Los bienes de la Iglesia en México (1856–1875)* (Mexico City: El Colegio de México, 1971); and Francisco López Camara, *La Estructura Económica y Social Durante la Época de la Reforma* (Mexico City: Siglo XXI, 1967), p. 198. López Camara (p. 210) quotes Binet, an official under French Minister Mantelon, as saying sales were affected not only to bring land into the market, but also to obtain capital, and they probably brought in 550 to 560 million pesos.

[2] Concerning this, see Bazant, *Los bienes*. In 1868 Juárez offered subsidies to a British company to complete and operate the line.

committed themselves to a program of modernization with distinct ideas and scope. In general, it aimed to overcome the obstacles impeding the free play of market forces so as to favor production and trade. This entailed the development of resources and their commercialization in the most dynamic and open foreign markets that reduced transportation costs permitted them to reach. The expansion of foreign trade brought with it, and simultaneously was stimulated by, the entry of foreign capital to mobilize domestic resources within a framework in which national capital was lacking.

It entailed, therefore, elimination of foreign and internal trade barriers and also of a multitude of closed local and regional markets in order to form one on a national level. Removing external barriers required tariff modifications which meant the elimination of protectionism. Domestic obstacles were to be removed by enforcing the provisions in the Constitution of 1857 regarding elimination of interstate customs duties. The national market would be achieved through a more decisive land policy, one which deprived Indian communes of their lands and which proved more successful than Juárez's program because of the establishment of an extended railway system, which expanded from 400 miles in 1876 to over 15,000 miles in 1910. The stabilization of the government structure, thus insuring a guarantee of investors' life and capital, was no minor element in successfully attracting a sizable amount of foreign capital. Government stability did not mean equal guarantees to the whole population, as liberal principles promised, but it did extend the government's guarantees to potential investors, considered the most respectable group.

The government-conducted monetary policy, the public debt, and the government policy of railroad subsidies promoted exports and the entry of capital. The same policies regarding the public debt and subsidies promoted, initially through direct government action, the establishment of the basic preconditions required for expansion of the domestic market and the infrastructure for transportation, in order to reduce production costs and create the necessary conditions for profitable direct investment, for which adequate incentives otherwise would be lacking. All of these policy mechanisms were much more complex and not always explicit nor totally developed, yet they were extremely important in creating adequate incentives which had been lacking previously to stimulate growth.[3] In this realm the government created external economies by broadening the market and offering incentives for direct investment which henceforth and only henceforth, were incorporated into the country in increasing proportions.

In any event, one can say that with this pattern of growth through trade Mexico underwent a period of great economic expansion. The GNP grew at a rate of 2.7 percent per year in the period of Díaz regime and the role of foreign trade was decisive in that expansion. Exports increased at a rate of 6.6 percent while imports increased by 4.6 percent. The massive entry of foreign capital also played a vital role.[4] Although the diverse features of this growth will be analyzed later on, some of its peculiarities are worth mentioning here:

1. The influence of foreign capital is a salient characteristic.

2. There did not occur, as in Peru or Cuba, a significant immigration from abroad to provide a labor supply. The relative scarcity of manpower was resolved by the availability of labor following the breakup of the Indian communal landholding system.

3. The role of foreign demand for minerals and raw materials was fundamental, and the significance of exports was decisive in terms of growth. Nevertheless, the role of the expanded domestic market was of no minor importance and, in the long run, was perhaps one of the most significant results of this stage of growth.

4. The specialization induced by foreign demand did not lead to a greater dependence on one product or on one crop, but to a greater diversification of production that, in turn, aided the modernization of the productive structure. This, perhaps, constitutes the most startling disparity with other growth patterns based on exports—the case of Cuba, for example.

5. Although, undoubtedly, the income which was sent abroad in payment of interest or to service the debt continued to be

[3] Concerning this, see Douglass C. North, "Location Theory and Regional Economic Growth," *Journal of Political Economy* 63 (June 1955), pp. 243–258 or in David L. McKee, Robert D. Dean, and William H. Leahy, *Regional Economics: Theory and Practice* (New York: The Free Press, 1970), pp. 29–48.

[4] Fernando Rosenzweig, "El Desarrollo Económico de México de 1877 a 1911," *El Trimestre Económico,* vol. 32, no. 127 (1965), p. 405.

significant, it may be assumed that, given the economy's characteristics, there existed certain multiplier effects so that a significant portion of the earnings derived from exports was distributed within the country.

6. The government adopted policies to bring out and take advantage of these characteristics.

As was mentioned earlier, these policies were not part of a program that had been conceived right from the beginning. They do, however, represent conscious and deliberate efforts, at least on the part of some key participants such as Matias Romero, three times minister of finance and Ivan de Limantour, undersecretary of finance and then minister after 1898. The government's policies will be analyzed on three related levels—protection of industry, fiscal or monetary considerations, and the burden of foreign debt. For example, a cheap money treasury policy resulted in a drop in imports, thereby transferring earnings to the more labor-intensive sector of domestic production, which meant somehow a relatively wider distribution of the national income. Now, let us see how this growth was accomplished in different sectors.

Railroads

As was previously indicated, the construction of a railway system to unite the numerous isolated local and regional markets was an indispensable prerequisite for the expansion of the market to a national level, particularly since Mexico is a country without a system of navigable rivers. Unlike those of the United States and Argentina, the Mexican railroad network was laid through territory where population and trade patterns were already established. These patterns were defined as early as the seventeenth and eighteenth centuries, when the mining economy had determined definite population patterns. An extended network of roads linked the *Reales de minas,* Zacatecas, San Luis, and Guanajuato, with the capital, Mexico City, and the latter with an outlet to the sea.[5]

[5] This pattern contrasts with that established in areas of the American hemisphere where a different economic pattern of exploitation exists, as agriculture was established near the coastal zones. See Caio Prado Junior, *Colonial Background of Modern Brazil* (Berkeley and Los Angeles, Calif.: University of California Press, 1967), pp. 31, 32.

The possibility of maintaining communication between scattered villages and isolated Indian communities depended, of course, on the activity which determined that population and trade pattern—mining. When mining declined, the entire system was interrupted, and these communities reverted to a state of self-sufficiency.[6] The decline of silver production and the wars and internal conflicts lasting from 1810 to 1870 heightened this isolation. The pattern of isolated population nuclei scattered widely throughout the interior of Mexico (a characteristic of mining economies) was complemented by two other coastal axes of settlement, on the Gulf of Mexico (agricultural and cotton producing areas and ports for exportation) and the Pacific (linked to Far Eastern trade) which were, to a great extent, independent of one another. To connect the scattered interior villages with those of the coast in order to establish a national market was the purpose of a policy which, though begun by Juárez, reached its culmination at the end of Díaz's first presidential term and continued during González's term from 1880 to 1884.[7]

With respect specifically to railway policy, two aspects bear consideration: the design of the railway network and the instruments for realizing that design, that is, whether it is to be accomplished by direct construction and administration by the federal government, by the various state governments, or by private management and under what conditions in each instance.

The basic objective of Mexican policies consisted in connecting the different regions of Mexico in an east-west direction, that is, to

[6] This has been thoroughly investigated in François Chevalier's excellent work, *Land and Society in Colonial Mexico* (Berkeley and Los Angeles, Calif.: University of California Press, 1966).

[7] This perhaps is the chief difference between the role of the railroads in Mexico and in Argentina. In Mexico previously inhabited areas had to be linked, thus making it necessary to superimpose their construction upon a structure that had been defined since colonial times. In Argentina, however, railroads were built in a demographic and social vacuum and thus defined new patterns of populating the area. Cf. Roberto Cortés Conde, "Tendencias en el Crecimiento de la Población Urbana en la Argentina," *Actas del 38 Congreso de Americanistas* (Stuttgart, Germany, 1968). It must be emphasized, however, that though railroads are established upon an existing structure, they modify the relative importance of each region in terms of the entire economy.

connect transversely the Gulf of Mexico with the Pacific Ocean, thus crossing and linking the villages en route. There was, on the other hand, great resistance to uniting the central area of greatest population density and importance with the northern zones bordering the United States. The memory of the War of 1848 was still vivid and undoubtedly influenced congressional reluctance to guarantee concessions to the northern region. They were probably still adhering to the advice attributed to Lerdo de Tejada, "Between strength and weakness it is best to have the desert in the middle." Despite this fear and the earlier construction of the Mexico-Veracruz railroad, resistance to United States influence buckled under the railroad craze of the 1880s. Díaz's forceful personality was no minor element in according concessions to railroad lines, which meant the extension of important United States railways into central Mexico which had reached the border only a short time before.

Although prevailing opinion favored private activity, Spanish legal tradition on the subject of public services influenced the government at the outset to participate directly in railroad operations. The direct efforts of the state had no great or enduring success because of the lack of mobile capital and an administrative structure which could handle the undertaking. The next stage in the evolution of government railroad policy consisted of offering concessions to those states which were interested in constructing railroads and which, in turn, were assured of federal subsidies. The first one granted was to the state of Guanajuato in 1887 for constructing a railway from Celaya to León.

During this phase, lasting from 1876 to 1880, of the twenty-eight concessions granted to twenty states, eight had to be canceled, while only twelve were allowed to continue. Of these, only eight actually did, and they made very little progress. By the time Díaz concluded his first term in 1880 only 226.5 kilometers of narrow gauge track had been laid.[8] In other instances local authorities speculating with concession rights, transferred concessions to private companies that were generally in no condition to undertake an operation of such dimensions and were, therefore,

[8] See Francisco R. Calderón, "Los Ferrocarriles," chap. 5, in Daniel Cosío Villegas, ed., *Historia Moderna de México,* vol. 7 (Mexico City: Ed. Hermes, 1965), p. 483.

beset with difficulties. The boom period in the establishment and expansion of the railway system unquestionably occurred during the brief González term, when lines constructed expanded from 400 miles in 1880 to about 3,000. Nevertheless, the general line of policy subsequently pursued was already defined by the concessions granted by the end of Díaz's first term.

These concessions opened the way for foreign investments which were offered all sorts of guarantees and assurances. Furthermore, it ended once and for all the isolation of the northern frontier. The North American companies that had reached El Paso and Laredo now found the opportunity propitious for extending their lines southward. This they did in a new rush which continued until the first decade of this century, at which point the Mexican government effected a substantial modification of its railway policy.

One of the most important lines was the Central Mexico Railway (Central), a company founded under Massachusetts laws and in which the interests of the Atchison, Topeka and Santa Fe Railroad predominated.[9] In record time—three years—it completed the line that linked Mexico City to the United States border at El Paso. In May 1880, for the first time in history, a train made the entire run from Mexico City to Chicago.

The other important group was the Nacional Mexicano in which the Denver–Río Grande Railroad held an interest. It had reached Laredo and from there extended as far as Monterrey and then on to Saltillo toward southern Mexico. Working north from Mexico City it reached Laredo in 1888. In May 1881 the Southern Pacific, dominated by Collins Huntington's strong personality, founded the Compañía Internacional de Construcciones Ferroviarias. El Internacional (International Mexican Railroad) linked San Antonio, El Paso, El Aguila, and El Torreón and connected with El Central. When Huntington died in 1901, it was transferred to El Nacional.

The English in 1888 founded the Interoceanic Company, which acquired a concession that had been granted in 1878 to the state of Morelos (Mexico-Morelos-Cuernavaca). In 1888 Interoceanic

[9] See Fred William Powell, *The Railroads of Mexico* (Boston: The Straford Company, 1921), pp. 127 et seq.

acquired the line connecting Mexico City, Puebla, Jalapa, and Veracruz. In 1889 it acquired the concession for the line to Acapulco. It must be noted that railroad interests were linked to the commercial interests of each investment group, which related to the markets of each. The railroad concessions presented overly complex problems for the Mexican government. Subsidy payments made in cash or in certificates from customs receipts were a heavy burden on government revenue and obliged the government to seek other sources of financing in order to meet these short-term debts. Another problem in the construction of the railroads was the disorganized design of the network: this in some areas resulted in a disorderly superimposition of several lines; in other areas there were none at all, or else tracks of different gauges were mixed without regard to criteria of uniformity. The manner in which railroad design contributed, or failed to contribute, to developing isolated regions and the role tariffs played in the railroad development were criticized in a report written in 1898 by Secretary of the Treasury, José Limantour. This helped to pass the Railroad Law of 1899, which stipulated precise conditions for governing railway policy and terminated the anarchy rampant in this field.

Rationalization led the government to a more decidedly interventionist policy. Limantour was gravely concerned with the enormous power concentrated in the railroad companies, a concern intensified by the demonstrable trend elsewhere in the economy toward concentration and absorption of the insolvent by the more efficient once the first boom had passed. Limantour sought a way to avoid private monopoly; he was convinced there was no alternative to establishing, to some extent, a government monopoly, and he managed to impose his own viewpoints on those of Díaz.

The sequence of transactions was more or less as follows: Interoceanic prior to 1887 controlled most of the stock of El Nacional. In 1901, after Collins Huntington's death, Internacional, with a huge deficit, surrendered an important portion of its shares, which were transferred to El Nacional. At that point in the early years of the twentieth century El Central was also in extremely difficult straits, and it seemed likely that El Nacional, by means of stock purchase, would obtain total control of the former. A veritable railroad monopoly was thus established, covering about two-thirds of the established lines in Mexico. In 1906, however, the government in a direct transaction purchased the stock of the Pierce group which held the majority of El Central. From then on, through its stock participation, it began to exert influence in the companies' control. From there to the ultimate consolidation of the Ferrocarriles Centrales into Ferrocarriles Nacionales de México with a government majority was a short step. This move was completed in 1909 with the establishment of a system of mixed companies with government participation along with private English and North American participation in which the former retained majority control. Eight thousand out of a total 13,000 miles thus remained under state control. Over 3,000 miles were controlled by independent companies. This system constituted a railroad network extending throughout Mexico in lines going from north to south and from the Atlantic to the Pacific and was a central factor in the economic growth of Mexico.

The railroad allowed the establishment of industries in zones removed from the centers of consumption or production and facilitated the expansion of the market by the radical reduction of heretofore high transportation costs. The cotton industry, formerly in Veracruz, then in Sonoma and Nuevo León, was one such. It was decisive also, as will be observed, in establishing the new mining industry that was linked to the most modern smelting processes.

The railroads spurred a modification in the relative importance of various regions. The northern zone, one of the first areas traversed by the railroads and enjoying greater proximity to the United States market and new centers of production such as Torreón, acquired particular importance, whereas other more traditional zones—Zacatecas, Pachuca, Guanajuato—declined.[10]

The importance of transportation was also reflected in the diversification of the structure of production and Mexican foreign trade which had heretofore been based on silver extraction. Mining production, which had depended solely on silver and precious metals, was extended to other industrial minerals (zinc, lead, copper). Changes in the mining industry demanded as a pre-

[10] Rosenzweig, "El Desarrollo."

requisite the existence of railroads, since they provided the necessary lower-cost transportation to the smelting centers (on the north bank of the Río Grande), but the entrance of foreign capital, which came from the United States, was also needed. This permitted the replacement by a more up-to-date smelting system of the *patio* system, a vestige of the colonial period. Robert Towne was one of the most influential promoters in the incorporation of North American capital, although until the period when oil became the principal export product (after 1910), no group attained the success or importance of the complex of Guggenheim interests which operated through various corporations.[11] Asarco (American Smelting and Refining Company), Guggenex, and even the family firm itself were active from 1890 on, when David Guggenheim was first introduced by Robert Towne to Díaz, with whom he subsequently maintained cordial relations. The first three foundries in Monterrey set up in 1892 were followed by others in Aguas Calientes in 1895, Sierra Mojada (Coahuila), Chihuahua, Baja California, and so forth. Guggenheim was not the only foreigner to invest in Mexico; others had appeared before him, such as the aforementioned Towne and later Phelps Dodge, Mac Elhyn, James Gardiner, Collins Huntington, and many others who responded to the incentives augured by the new Mexican phase and more specifically to the new law of 1892. This law ended predominant government control over subsoil property, the Spanish patrimonial criterion that had been the traditional rule of ownership since colonial times and that had been ratified by laws in 1783 and 1884.

Under the new regime, mining would be privately operated, the minerals of the soil belonging to the owners of the property. The aforementioned legislation established specific rules regarding claims on mineral deposits and allowed ample freedom for exploration. As soon as hindrances were removed from the exploration, acquisition, and exploitation of the subsoil, capital flowed in freely, providing a great impetus to mining activity.

[11] For a detailed account of the activity of North American capital in the mining industry, see Marvin D. Bernstein, *Mexican Mining Industry* (Albany, N.Y.: State University of New York, 1964).

TABLE 5–1 MINING PRODUCTION IN MEXICO, 1891, 1900, 1910

	Silver (kilograms)	Gold (kilograms)	Lead (tons)	Zinc (tons)	Copper (tons)
1891	1,087,261	1,477	30,187	—	5,650
1900	1,776,410	12,697	63,828	1,100	22,473
1910	2,416,669	41,420	124,292	1,833	48,160

SOURCE: Bernstein, *Mexican Mining Industry,* p. 51.

TABLE 5–2 CAPITAL INVESTMENTS IN MINES AND REFINERIES ACCORDING TO OWNER'S NATIONALITY (*in millions of dollars*)

	USA	France	UK	Mexican	Others
Mines	223.0	5.0	43.6	7.5	7.8
Refineries	26.5	—	—	7.0	3.0

SOURCE: Marion Letcher, "Wealth of Mexico," *Daily Consular and Trade Reports,* July 1912, cited in in Luis N. D'Olwer, *"Las inversiones extranjeras,"* chap. 10 in Cosío Villegas, *Historia Moderna de México,* vol. 8, pp. 1140 et seq.

Tables 5–1 and 5–2 reveal the evolution of production and the changes in various categories.

The changes in mining were accompanied by a notable diversification of production in the economy generally. In 1898 60 percent of the exports consisted of precious metals; by 1910 these had diminished to 46 percent, with the category sundry items covering the remaining 54 percent. In 1877–1878 silver alone accounted for 60 percent of the value of all exports. By 1910–1911 it was reduced to 33 percent; hemp, coffee, sugar, rubber, and livestock rose in importance in the country's exports.

This phenomenon applied not only to export products. There was also progress in industries geared to the domestic market. The cotton and textile industries in general and food and beverage industries (especially beer), were some outstanding examples. The physical volume of production doubled between 1878 and 1911,

TABLE 5–3 SEVERAL MEXICAN EXPORTS
(*in percentages of total volume exported*)

	1877–1878	1893–1894	1910–1911
Hemp	16.8	27.8	18.6
Coffee	13.7	19.0	5.8
Sugar	2.8	0.2	—
Cattle	0.3	0.2	3.6
Rubber	0.3	0.2	9.9
Copper	—	9.0	12.5
Lead	—	—	5.3

SOURCE: In Rosenzweig, "El Comercio Exterior," chap. 6 in Cosío Villegas, *Historia Moderna de México,* vol. 7, p. 671. [The statistics are from *Estadísticas Económicas del Porfiriato. Comercio Exterior de México 1877–1911* (Mexico City: El Colegio de México, 1960).]

TABLE 5–4 IMPORTS OF CONSUMER AND CAPITAL GOODS
(*in percentages of total imports*)

	1877–1878	1910–1911
Consumer Goods	75	43
Capital Goods	25	57

SOURCE: Rosenzweig, "El Comercio Exterior," pp. 690, 694.

by a cumulative annual rate of 3.6 percent.[12] In the period between 1894 and 1901 the textile industry grew at an annual rate of 5.3 percent. Although that rate was not matched by the consumer goods industries category as a whole, this is due to their being supplanted in importance by other capital goods industries related to mining development, transportation, and urban activity (chemical products, construction, iron and steel).[13] Thus, an

[12] Rosenzweig, "La Industria," chap. 4 in Cosío Villegas, *Historia Moderna de México,* vol. 7, p. 325.

[13] Ibid., pp. 328, 329.

TABLE 5–5 GROSS NATIONAL PRODUCT OF MEXICO, 1895–1910
(*in 1950 pesos*)

	Agriculture	Cattle	Mining	Oil	Manufacturing	Total
1895	2,107	850	431	—	806	8,863
1900	1,991	907	541	—	1,232	9,861
1905	2,543	1,017	848	1	1,475	12,460
1910	2,692	1,020	1,022	19	1,663	13,524

SOURCE: *Enrique Pérez López,* "The National Product of Mexico, 1895 to 1964," in Pérez López et al., *Mexico's Recent Economic Growth* (Austin, Tex.: University of Texas Press, 1967), p. 28.

early process of import substitution appears, reinforcing the growth of domestic industrial production in the country.

This growth was general across the entire economy, although in different proportions in each major sector.

It is evident from the preceding table that although agriculture rose, its rate of growth was slower than the economy as a whole, while the growth rate of cattle was even slower. On the other hand, mining and manufacturing (the latter is not an export activity) rose at a greater rate than the overall rate of the economy. This would indicate, to a certain extent at least, that the rhythm of growth of export activity was maintained by the domestic sector of the economy.[14]

EXPORTS

Exports were the most dynamic factor in the economy's growth. In current pesos, exports increased eight-and-a-half-fold between 1877 and 1910, while in volume they increased a little over seven times. In dollars this comes to only four-and-a-half times: the

[14] With regard to the Chilean case, see Clark Reynolds, "Development Problems of an Export Economy," in Markos Mamalakis and Clark Reynolds, *Essays on the Chilean Economy* (Homewood, Ill.: Richard Irwin, 1965).

TABLE 5–6 VALUE OF MEXICAN EXPORTS
(millions of current pesos and index numbers, 1877–1910)
(Base 1900:100)

Year	Value	I.N.
1877	32.6	20
1880	41.0	25
1890	67.9	42
1900	160.7	100
1910	281.2	175

SOURCE: *Estadísticas Económicas del Porfiriato*, p. 75.

TABLE 5–7 EXPORT OF GOODS AND PRECIOUS METALS IN THE TOTAL OF MEXICAN EXPORTS
(in millions of Mexican pesos)

	Goods	Precious Metals	Total
1877	6.9	25.7	32.6
1880	10.6	30.4	41.0
1890	24.9	43.0	67.9
1900	67.3	93.4	160.7
1910	150.8	130.4	281.2

SOURCE: *Estadísticas Económicas del Porfiriato*, p. 75.

difference can be explained by the devaluation of Mexican silver currency during the same period.[15]

Industrial goods and minerals, the sector that one might call modern, grew at a greater rate than that of precious minerals.

Within the category of precious metals the growth of gold was much greater than that of silver.

15 In millions of dollars: 1877, 29.6; 1880, 36.5; 1890, 56.8; 1900, 78.4; and 1910, 140.

TABLE 5–8 EXPORTS OF GOLD AND SILVER
(*in millions of Mexican pesos*)

	Gold	Silver
1888–1889	0.9	41.3
1895	11.3	61.0
1900	19.1	74.3
1905	36.4	75.6
1910	49.4	80.8

SOURCE: *Estadísticas Económicas del Porfiriato*, p. 77.

MONETARY POLICY AND FOREIGN TRADE

The monetary policy adopted by the economic authorities played a decisive role in promoting export activity. It was based on a deliberate attempt to devalue the Mexican peso in terms of foreign currency (which does not mean a loss of purchasing power of the domestic currency, which is something else) in order to promote Mexican exports in a period of a downward trend of international prices lasting until the end of the century. Its purpose was also to reduce imports by raising the value of foreign currency.

Mexican currency was based on the silver standard and consisted of the silver peso (a unit of 27.073 grams 0.902). There was no paper money aside from common bank bills. In reference to the Mexican monetary system, one of the prominent figures of economic policy declared:

> Mexico is legally a bi-metallic country because we have free coinage of both gold and sliver at the ratio of sixteen to one, but practically we are a silver mono-metallic country because under the operation of the Gresham Law all the gold bullion and the gold coin existing in Mexico is exported as merchandise, and silver is the only metallic money used there in payment of debts or for any other purpose.[16]

Romero went on to state that Mexico's reasons for adhering to silver usage were not arbitrary. In the first place, Mexico was the

[16] Matías Romero, *The Silver Standard in Mexico* (New York: The Knickerbocker Press, 1898), pp. 594, 595–596. Romero was minister of the treasury under Juárez and later under Díaz.

most important silver producer in the world: two-thirds of the world's supply came from Mexican mines. In pointing out that Mexico maintained a system of free convertibility without using paper currency, he supported his argument by also referring to a report on the silver standard made by the Japanese government which specifically stated that the silver standard presented among other advantages the following: imports were discouraged because of the high price of goods from foreign countries employing the gold standard; and exports were encouraged, since their costs were defrayed in silver, which were considerably less in relations to the costs in countries employing the gold standard, due to silver's lower value.

This fact was clearly noted by contemporary observers and was undoubtedly one of the factors in encouraging exports and investment of foreign capital. In *Facts and Figures about Mexico,* a report published by the Mexican Central Railway Bureau of Information, and cited by Romero, the following observation was made:

> The premium on gold has been the cause of immense internal improvement throughout the country. The capital kept at home has been invested in irrigation schemes, in improving large tracts of fallow land, and in other enterprises of a like character. The premium also brought much foreign capital here which has been invested in various branches of industry, particularly in the production of articles of exportation. The foreign investor doubles his capital when he brings it to Mexico. He gets the advantage of cheap and docile labor for silver and sells his exported product for gold.[17]

Thus while silver suffered a very serious devaluation (the 16/1 silver/gold ratio dropped to 32/1 in 1910 for reasons totally divorced from the Mexican balance of payments), domestic prices and salaries for the same period remained more or less stable. The premium on gold provided an additional benefit to the exporter who obtained a greater quantity of silver, with a more or less similar domestic purchasing power, for the same amount of gold, the currency used in international transactions. The devaluation of silver did more than provide support for the export sector. It promoted the entry of foreign capital which, when changed into domestic currency, increased its original capital through devalua-

17 Ibid., pp. 570–571.

TABLE 5–9 VALUE OF A MEXICAN PESO
(*in U.S. dollars*)

1872	1.001
1878	0.910
1883	0.882
1888	0.759
1893	0.657
1898	0.448

SOURCE: Rosenzweig, "La Industria," p. 866.

tion. Finally, by maintaining free convertibility at a fictitious legal rate silver producers were aided in obtaining gold through the government with a much smaller quantity of silver than would be needed on the open market. Thus, while exporters were not obliged to sell gold at the legal rate and sold it both within and outside the country at the prevailing international market price, producers were able to sell silver to the government at the legal rate which was much higher (for silver) than the market rate.

With respect to foreign trade, it is noteworthy that since the value of the domestic silver currency was not a variable dependent upon foreign trade balances nor on domestic price relation, but rather on world supply and demand for the product which Mexican trade did not affect, Mexico was able to maintain during the entire period under study a favorable balance of trade with no change in the valuation of its currency (in silver).[18] As may be observed, the application of this mechanism was a deliberate instrument to promote the influx of foreign capital, to stimulate exports, and to discourage imports.

The Mexican silver peso underwent the devaluation shown in Table 5–9 in relation to the dollar between 1872 and 1898, the same devaluation as that of silver itself.

The advantages gained in the export sector can be deduced by

[18] The silver devaluation resulted primarily from demonetization. See A. Sauerbeck, "Prices of Commodities and the Precious Metals" in E. M. Carus Wilson, *Essays in Economic History*, vol. 3 (London: Edward Arnold, 1966), p. 78.

TABLE 5–10 EXPORTS
(*in millions of pesos and in millions of dollars*)

Year	Pesos	Dollars
1877–1878	32.16	29.6
1880–1881	41.10	36.5
1890–1891	67.9	56.8
1900–1901	160.7	78.4

SOURCE: *Estadísticas Económicas del Porfiriato*, pp. 75 and 152.

comparing the amount of exports in pesos or in dollars in Table 5–10.

Thus, though there was barely any difference in 1877 between earnings in Mexican pesos and in dollars and only a slight difference in the following years, the situation changed completely by the end of the century, when the income in Mexican pesos was, in fact, double that earned in dollars. If the domestic price variation was not appreciable, the extra profit from the export sector (the gold premium) must have been considerable. Other data concerning prices provided by Rosenzweig tend to support this.

Nominal salaries between 1877 and 1898 increased by about 54 percent. This would mean that real salaries increased by 18.5 percent, while the price of foreign currency, in which exports were paid, increased by 89 percent. Romero considered salaries to have remained stable during the entire period (at approximately 35 cents per day), but this did not mean a drop in real salaries since the price level remained stable.[19]

If the increase in the value of the dollar is compared to domestic prices and salaries, as in Table 5–11, it is apparent that the export sector was the principal beneficiary of the devaluation of silver.

One may deduce from the evolution of prices and salaries and the peso-dollar rate that the internal purchasing power of the currency decreased much less than its external devaluation and that real salaries had apparently improved. This provided an important

[19] Matías Romero, *Mexico and the United States*, vol. 1 (New York: G. P. Putnam's Sons, 1898), p. 529.

TABLE 5–11 DOLLAR VALUE IN RELATION TO THE PESO
(*prices and salaries in index numbers*)
(*base 1877:100*)

		Rate	
Year	*Dollar–Peso Rate*	*Prices*	*Salaries*
1877	100	100	100
1898	189	126	103

SOURCE: *Estadísticas Económicas del Porfiriato,* p. 153, for the dollar-peso rates, and Rosenzweig, "Moneda y Bancos," chap. 8 in Cosío Villegas, *Historia Moderna de México,* p. 868, for prices and salaries.

incentive for exports, which obtained better prices because of the higher price of gold at the time of a declining price trend in world markets which continued until the end of the nineteenth century.

The decline of silver reached its lowest point around 1898. After 1902–1903 a period of monetary instability commenced, followed by a slight revaluation of the Mexican peso. This is shown in Table 5–12.

Instability affected commercial transactions which were subject to unforeseeable fluctuations. The revaluation of the Mexican peso, if allowed to continue, could have meant a considerable loss for the export sector. Finally, it must not be forgotten that although for foreign capital the devaluation of silver was advantageous when foreigners had to convert their capital in gold (or gold standard currency) into silver since this was automatically doubled, the same did not apply when the inverse process occurred, that is, when silver pesos had to be converted into gold (or foreign currency) in order to remit profits to their countries of origin.

All of these reasons, but particularly the urgent need to obtain stability in the market, led to the monetary reform of 1905. The law of March 1905 established a bimetallic standard, retaining the silver peso of 27.073 grams at the 0.9027 standard but establishing its equivalence at 75 centigrams of gold or an equivalent of 0.50 United States dollars, thereby legally accepting the devaluation which the currency had in reality already undergone. The

TABLE 5–12 VALUE OF THE PESO, 1898–1905
(*in dollars*)

Fiscal Years	Value of the Peso	Annual Percentage of Change
1897	0.448	—
1898–1899	0.472	—
1899–1900	0.476	0.8
1900–1901	0.488	2.5
1901–1902	0.441	−9.7
1902–1903	0.398	−9.8
1903–1904	0.441	10.8
1904–1905	0.483	9.5

SOURCE: *Estadísticas Económicas del Porfiriato,* p. 152.

reform was aided by a brief period of silver valuation lasting from 1906 to 1907, which allowed Mexico to export a considerable quantity of white metal in order to purchase gold, the basis of the new monetary system. Mexico was thereby incorporated into the club of nations that assumed the obligation of maintaining currency stability in relation to gold and gained financial prestige in international markets, though the effects of this measure on trade were and continue to be debated. According to Rosenzweig,

> In contrast to what had occurred prior to 1905, when gold prices of exports as well as imports tended to decline while silver prices rose, a favorable effect noted by Matias Romero, after that year both gold and silver prices, united now by the monetary reform, shared the same lot: declining exports and rising imports. The foreign sector of the economy thus lost much of its dynamism which had been one of the decisive factors in the development attained thus far. This may be observed in the decrease in the value of exports after 1905.[20]

CAPITAL INVESTMENT

It was stated previously that one of the prerequisites for initiating exploitation of an export-oriented resource (in this case as well

20 Rosenzweig, "La Industria," p. 885.

TABLE 5–13 DEVELOPMENT OF FOREIGN TRADE
(*in index numbers*)
(*base 1900–01:100*)

	Exports		**Imports**	
	Prices in:		*Prices in:*	
Years	*Silver*	*Gold*	*Silver*	*Gold*
1877–1878	51.2	95.5	74.5	138.9
1883–1884	53.5	95.9	74.2	133.0
1887–1888	65.9	102.5	79.9	124.2
1892–1893	68.3	91.9	85.8	115.5
1897–1898	82.1	75.4	98.5	90.4
1900–1901	100.0	100.0	100.0	100.0
1903–1904	116.1	104.9	112.0	101.2
1905–1906	116.7	121.3	102.6	105.1
1908–1909	107.8	109.8	102.7	104.5
1910–1911	105.3	107.7	112.7	115.0

SOURCE: Rosenzweig, "Moneda y Bancos" (the data are from *Estadísticas Económicas del Porfiriato,* pp. 63, 72, 96, and 108).

as others) was capital, a factor that, though not totally lacking in Mexico, was at least scarce. For the evolution of foreign investments there exist isolated and not always comparable data, though the best of these refer, of course, to the cases of British and North American investments.

In 1883 North American investments in Mexico were estimated at 30 million dollars. In less than twenty years they rose to 501.6 million (1902), and in the brief nine-year period ending in 1911 they doubled and reached 1,057.8 million dollars. English investments were 32.7 million pounds in 1880 and rose to almost 90 million pounds in 1910, a much smaller increase than that for North American investments. Nevertheless, the analysis ought to be made in two distinct periods. The first period lasted until the close of the nineteenth century, when investment doubled from 32.7 million pounds in 1880 to 65.4 million pounds in 1900. A second, quite distinct period begins after 1900 when the increase in British investments was slower and corresponded precisely to predomi-

TABLE 5–14 BRITISH INVESTMENTS IN MEXICO
(*in millions of pounds*)

Year	Public Debt	Direct Investments	Total
1880	23.5	9.2	32.7
1890	20.7	39.2	59.9
1900	25.0	40.4	65.4
1910	8.2	79.4	87.6
1911	13.4	50.9	64.3

SOURCE: For 1880, 1890, and 1900, J. Fred Rippy, *British Investments in Latin America 1822–1949* (Minneapolis, Minn.: University of Minnesota Press, 1959), and J. Fred Rippy, *The United States and Mexico* (New York: Crofts, 1926). For 1910, *Statist*. For 1911, Letcher, *Wealth of Mexico,* quoted by Luis N. D'Olwer, "Las Inversiones Extranjeras," in Cosío Villegas, *Historia Moderna de México,* vol. 8, p. 1141.

nance of United States capital which was then in the process of displacing European investments.

The distribution of British investments is shown in Table 5–14.

The orientation of British investments was initially toward the public sector, effected through bonds of the public debt, and the shift is indicative of a general change in the nature and direction of foreign investments. At the beginning of the period under consideration, 60 percent of the foreign capital entering Mexico was invested in bonds of the public debt, while the remaining 40 percent was in direct investments. The relations between both present a further complication, since the estimated amount of the bonds is trustworthy, while the figure for direct investments is more or less approximate. Around 1900, however, 86 percent of foreign capital was placed in direct investments, while only 14 percent was in bonds of the public debt. One may, therefore, deduce that, as in other sectors of the economy, the policy of attracting foreign capital was divided into two distinct periods. In the initial phase, prior to expansion of the market, when the country lacked a modern economy, railroads, transportation, industries, and so forth, adequate incentives for the investment of foreign capital

TABLE 5–15 NORTH AMERICAN INVESTMENTS IN 1902
(*in millions of U.S. dollars*)

Railroads	335.1
Mines	102.0
Real Estate Holdings	32.7
Industry	10.2
Trade	8.2
Banks	7.3
Public Services	6.0
Petroleum	0.1
Total	501.6

SOURCE: A.D. Barlow, "United States Enterprises in Mexico" in *Commercial Relations of the United States with Foreign Countries during the Year 1902* (Washington, D.C., Government Printing Office, 1905), pp. 433–503, quoted by D'Olwer, "Las Inversiones Extranjeras," p. 1133.

were absent, despite the fact that the scarce capital available in the area commanded high returns, because of the narrow size of the market. In such a situation only a government capable of guaranteeing solvency and respect for obligations that had been contracted could channel investments. The government itself had to undertake the quest for funds for essential works or else, in specific undertakings like railroads, guarantee a safe, minimum benefit to investors. Given the lack of information on conditions in Mexico and the great misgivings on the part of European investors regarding the feasibility of direct investments, only the formal commitment of a financially "respectable" government could offer some attraction to investors provided, of course, that a higher rate of return was offered than the prevailing rate in Europe. This indicates that foreign investors had no greater spirit of risk than local investors.

In the second phase, through market expansion and an infrastructure of transportation and communications which assured lower costs for production, the basic prerequisites were met, and the market offered sufficient incentives for the direct flow of capital

TABLE 5–16 NORTH AMERICAN INVESTMENTS IN MEXICO, 1911
(*in millions of U.S. dollars*)

Railroads	644.4
Mines and Metallurgy	249.5
Public Debt	52.0
Real Estate	40.7
Banks	34.6
Petroleum	15.0
Industry	11.4
Trade	4.7
Various	4.8
Total	1,057.1

SOURCE: Letcher, *Wealth of Mexico,* quoted by D'Olwer, "Foreign Investments," p. 1135.

investments in activities which now offered even greater expectations of profit.

Therefore, the initial phase was marked by the necessity of an active policy of contracting debts in the public sector which looked to international markets to obtain through credit the capital that the country lacked for construction of essential works. In the second phase, concomitant with the changes noted in the composition of British investments and the growth in importance of North American investments, there was a change toward those sectors preferred by North American investors.

In 1902 Consul Barlow's report estimated United States investments at 501.6 million dollars, divided as shown in Table 5–15.

In 1911, North American investments, which reached 1,057.1 million dollars, were divided as shown in Table 5–16.

English investments in 1910 reached 87 million pounds (435 million dollars). The largest proportion was in railroads, with smaller amounts in public services, mines, real estate holdings, and the public debt. The distribution is shown in Table 5–17.

It is evident from Tables 5–15, 5–16, and 5–17 that railroads were the most important investment for Americans and Englishmen followed by mining, the public debt, banks, and real estate

TABLE 5–17 BRITISH INVESTMENTS IN MEXICO AT THE END OF 1910
(*in thousands of pounds sterling*)

	Pounds Sterling
Government (Public Debt)	6,653,000
Municipal (Loans)	1,623,000
Railroads	54,304,000
Banks	1,576,000
Commercial and Industrial Companies	1,875,000
Electric Light and Power	937,000
Land	7,416,000
Mines	7,440,000
Petroleum	998,000
Rubber	1,683,000
Tramways	2,827,000
Total	87,332,000

SOURCE: Carlos Díaz Dufoo, *México y los capitales extranjeros* (Paris: Charles Bourel, 1918), p. 421.

holdings. By 1911 petroleum had already appeared, although it had not yet reached the place it would later occupy. Further on the public debt is analyzed in detail.

With respect to subsequent additional investments, there exists the following data cited by Díaz Dufoo:[21]

	Pounds Sterling
1911	2,649,900
1912	4,085,700
1913	10,641,500

French investments rose to about 2,444 million francs, distributed as shown in Table 5–18.

In order to show a complete panorama of foreign investments in Mexico in the Porfirio Díaz period, Tables 5–19 and 5–20 have been drawn up.

21 See Carlos Díaz Dufoo, *México y los capitales extranjeros* (Paris: Charles Bourel, 1918), p. 422. Data of different sources are not comparable in general and should be considered only illustrative.

TABLE 5–18 FRENCH INVESTMENTS
(*in francs*)

	Values Quoted in the Paris Market
State Funds	656,891,776
Stocks—Banks, Railroads, Industrial and Mining Companies	1,013,510,000
Obligations—Mexican Territorial, Mortgage Banking, Development Banking and Real Estate, Banking, National Railroads, etc.	247,491,200
Certificates and Shares—National Bank, Inguarán Negotiation, Boleo, etc.	35,839,000
Total	1,953,731,916

	Values Quoted in Other Markets or Not Quoted
Financial Business	27,424,900
Industrial, Agricultural Companies, Railroads and Others	190,591,000
Mining	32,022,000
Coal Companies	12,260,000
Petroleum Companies	5,100,000
Other Companies	10,000,000
Obligations	50,537,500
Investments in Other Operations Not Covered in This or the Previous Table	162,500,000
Total	490,435,400

SOURCE: Díaz Dufoo, *México y los capitales extranjeros,* p. 425.

THE PUBLIC DEBT

The precondition for placing government bonds in the European market was the adjustment with European creditors of long-standing unpaid accounts, which varied in their characteristics and amounts. Employing realistic criteria, Mexican negotiators accepted some claims and rejected others, such as those that had been assumed and recognized under Maximilian's rule. Finally in 1883 a congressional law authorized the consolidation of the

TABLE 5–19 FOREIGN CAPITAL INVESTED IN MEXICO
(*in thousands of dollars*)

	1903	1907	1908	1910
United States	26.426[a]	354.248[b]	336.991[e]	—
		800.000[c]		
		1.200.000[d]		
		1.000.000[d]		
Great Britain	16.571[a]	264.236[b]	—	436.660[f]
France	4.145[a]	16.991[b]	—	—
Germany	11[a]	27.454[b]	—	—
Spain	—	12.334[b]	—	—
Austria-Hungary	—	400[b]	—	—
Italy	—	60[b]	—	—

[a] *Subcommission of the Monetary Congress, 1903. (These figures correspond only to investments in agricultural, mining, industrial, banking, and other companies—the first category in Table 5–20—and exclude railroads, public debt, and insurance. The figures do not coincide exactly due to the type of exchange used when the conversions were made.)*
[b] *Dirección de Estadística published a study in 1908 on* Movimiento de Sociedades Mineras y Mercantiles *according to inscription in the Registro Público y de Comercio, corresponding to the period from 1886 to 1907.*
[c] *W. O. Hornaday,* Moody's Magazine, *June 1907.*
[d] *Statistics of the United States.*
[e] Engineering and Mining Journal, *vol. 85.*
[f] Statist *of London at the end of 1910, in a table reproduced by* El economista mexicano, *January 1911.*

SOURCE: Díaz Dufoo, *México y los capitales extranjeros.* Values are cited in the currency of each country. The author effected the conversion to dollars according to the following exchange rates: 1 pound = 5 dollars; 1 franc, 1 peseta, and 1 lira = .20 dollars; 1 mark = .25 dollars; and 1 florin = .40 dollars.

foreign debt, and in 1888 this was accomplished by Minister Dublan following lengthy and prolonged negotiations.

Mexico's obligations, which amounted to 23,343.270 pounds sterling (116.5 millions Mexican pesos or dollars), were reduced to 14,626.279 pounds sterling by the savings achieved with the 1888 Dublan conversion.[22] This is shown in Table 5–21.

[22] It is however a significant sum when compared with that of exports which in 1880 rose to 48.7 million pesos. The total sum of the debt was 73 million Mexican pesos and the service of the debt only 10 percent of total exports.

TABLE 5–20 FOREIGN INVESTMENTS IN MEXICO BY SECTORS
(*in thousands of dollars*)

Sectors	Total Foreign Investments[a]	United States[b]	Great Britain[c]
	1903	*1907*	*1910*
Agriculture, Mining, Industry, Banking and Others	54.171	—	123.760
Insurance	6.722	—	—
Railroads	305.326	400.000	271.520
Public Debt	172.142	—	33.265
Municipal Loans	—	—	8.115
Total	538.361	800.000[d]	436.660

[a] *Subcommission of the Monetary Congress, 1903.*
[b] *W. O. Hornaday,* Moody's Magazine, *June 1907.*
[c] Statist *of London, 1910, in a table reproduced by* El economista mexicano, *January 1911.*
[d] *The other items are not mentioned.*

SOURCE: Díaz Dufoo, *México y los capitales extranjeros,* chap. 13. Values are cited in the currency of each country. The author effected the conversion to dollars according to the following exchange rates: 1 Mexican peso = 0.398 dollars in 1903 and 1 sterling pound = 5 dollars in 1910.

In order to undertake payment of the consolidated debt plus the floating debt, the government obtained a loan from the firms of Bleichroeder and A. Gibbs & Sons for a nominal total value of 10.5 million pounds at an interest rate of 6 percent. Of this amount, 3.7 million pounds were immediately underwritten and traded in the market at 70 percent, which yielded an actual amount of 2,590,000 pounds. Deducting 110,000 for commissions, the remainder, 2,480,000 pounds, was consigned to payment of the floating debt. As for the remaining 6.8 million pounds, an option was offered to the firms of Bleichroeder and A. Gibbs & Sons, who endorsed bonds for 86.5 percent of their nominal value. Part of the funds obtained in this manner was devoted to payment of the consolidated debt. These maneuvers were not sufficient to get the government out of financial straits, for it had to pay short-term credits, particularly railroad subsidies, which had to be met in

TABLE 5–21 MEXICAN PUBLIC DEBT BEFORE AND AFTER THE 1888 DUBLAN CONVERSION
(*in thousands of pounds sterling*)

	Credits before Conversion	Admitted Proportion Percentage	Debt after Conversion
1851 Conversion	10,241.6	—	10,241.6
1851 Interest	6,145.0	15	921.7
1864 3 Percent Bonds	4,864.8	50	2,432.4
1837 5 Percent Bonds	434.4	20	86.9
3 Percent Certificates, 1851 Conversion	180.0	20	36.0
1886 Certificates (Baring)	75.5	20	15.1
1843 Bonds	200.0	29	58.0
1851 British Conversion Bonds	1,180.5	—	823.7
1846 5 Percent Bonds	21.5	—	10.7
Total	23,343.3		14,626.3

SOURCE: Jean Bazant, *Historia de la Deuda Exterior de México (1823–1946)* (Mexico City: El Colegio de México, 1968), p. 123.

cash by means of certificates granting the holder the right to collect customs revenue. This created grave problems in the administration of public finances, and the government thereafter lost the income from that source.

To end its financial embarrassment, the government decided to replace its short-term obligations with a new loan of 6 million pounds, which was also negotiated through the firm of Bleichroeder, at 88.75 percent of its nominal value, which amounted to an actual subscription, less commissions, of 5,325,000 pounds sterling in Mexican pesos (or 26.6 million dollars). This was used to pay 19.8 million to Central, 3.5 million to Mexicano R.R., 1.3 million to the National Construction Company, and 0.6 to Interoceanic, a total of 25.2 million, taking commissions into account. Combined with new loans, the public debt in 1893 came to a total of 19.1 million pounds (or 95.5 million dollars or Mexican pesos at nominal rate), the distribution of which is shown in Table 5–22.

TABLE 5–22 PUBLIC DEBT IN 1893
(*in thousands of pounds*)

Conversion 1888	6 percent	10,443
Tehuantepec Railroad	5 percent	2,700
Railroads, 1890	6 percent	5,983
Total		19,126

SOURCE: E. Turlington, *Mexico and Her Foreign Creditors* (New York: Columbia University Press, 1930), p. 220.

The amount of public debt, converted into Mexican pesos, was 95,635,000 pesos. If the domestic debt of 69 million Mexican pesos is added to this, it brings the total debt to 164.6 million Mexican pesos.

In 1893 the government was authorized to issue a new loan for 2.5 million pounds in order to meet payment of the floating debt. Another credit was negotiated through the firm of Bleichroeder for 3 million pounds. Of this, 1,650,000 pounds were actually taken up, and an option was left on the remaining 900,000 pounds. Six percent was paid, and the amount actually received was 60 percent of the face value of the bonds.

Toward the end of the century the economic stability and progress that had been attained emboldened the government to attempt a delicate experiment: the refunding or conversion of the foreign debt payable in gold in order to reduce the excessive burden on fiscal revenues which exorbitant interest rates had signified. The high interest rates had been motivated by expectations of insecurity. When, despite the crises of 1891 and 1893, Mexico was able to meet its obligations, this stimulated investors' confidence. By 1897 conditions were propitious for the refunding. After several overtures and negotiations, including some interesting approaches from North American banking firms, the 1899 conversion was made, though not directly with North Americans (though the latter participated in the conversion of 1899 as partners in European banking), through Bleichroeder Deutsche Bank, Dreschner, and J. P. Morgan. In order to effect the conver-

TABLE 5–23 FOREIGN PUBLIC DEBT 1900
(*in thousands of pounds sterling*)

6 Percent Loan	1888	36.1
6 Percent Loan	1890	7.3
6 Percent Loan	1893	0.6
5 Percent Tehuantepec by Loan	1889	53.7
5 Percent Loan	1899	23,628.9
Interest Accrued on These Loans		309.1
Total		24,035.7

SOURCE: Turlington, *Mexico and Her Foreign Creditors,* p. 229. £ = 5 Mexican pesos.

sion, a loan of 22.7 million pounds was contracted at an interest rate of 5 percent. The government pledged 62 percent of its customs revenues as a guarantee for the loan.[23]

The first 13 million pounds negotiated were taken up at 96 percent, while the remaining 9.71 million were taken up at 97.25 percent, from which 1 percent commission had to be deducted. This indicated greater confidence in Mexico in the international markets. Mexico's foreign debt at the turn of the century thereby rose to 24 million pounds sterling, the major portion of which corresponded to the refunding debt at 5 percent. The reduction in interest rate resulted in the savings of an appreciable sum, as Table 5–23 indicates.

In dollars the foreign debt was at that point 115 million United States dollars, a rather steep figure considering that total United States investments amounted to slightly over 500 million dollars.[24]

The final phase in the debt adjustment now remains to be described, and in this phase the nationalization of the railroads played an important role. In 1904 a loan for 40 million dollars was obtained in order to pay for the stocks and debentures of the railroad firms that the government had acquired in a vast operation conducted by Limantour in an attempt to break the railroad

[23] See Bazant, *Historia de la Deuda Exterior.*

[24] There is a notable difference between Rippy's and Turlington's figures. For 1900 Rippy figures English investments in bonds of public debt at 125 million dollars, while Turlington estimates a comprehensive total of 115 million.

TABLE 5–24 FOREIGN PUBLIC DEBT IN 1911
(*in thousands of Mexican pesos*)

Bonds of 1888, 1889, 1890 and 1893	23
5 Percent Bonds of 1889 Mexico City	15,753
5 Percent Bonds from the 1899 Conversion	103,856
4 Percent Bonds from the Railroad Loan of 1904	76,681
4 Percent Bonds from the 1910 Conversion	106,664
Total	302,977*

SOURCE: Bazant, *Historia de la Deuda Exterior,* p. 168.

* without debts of the railroads for 138,726,467 Mexican pesos.

TABLE 5–25 PUBLIC DEBT BETWEEN 1851 AND 1910
(*in millions of dollars and pounds sterling*)

	1850	**1888**	**1888 Conv.**	**1893**	**1900**	**1910**
Pounds	10.2	23.3	14.6	19.1	23.0	30.0
Dollars	51.0	116.5	73.0	95.5	115.0	150.0

SOURCE: Bazant, *Historia de la Deuda Exterior,* pp. 71, 123, 143, 155, and 169.

monopoly and nationalize railroad companies. These securities were contracted on the market at 89 percent. In 1910 a new conversion was carried out which permitted a reduction of the interest rate to 4 percent. The state of the external public debt by the end of the Porfirio Díaz period is indicated in Table 5–24.[25]

When converted to the new dollar parity, the public debt totaled 151 million dollars or 30 million pounds sterling.

The evolution of the public debt (in dollars and pounds sterling) since 1851 is shown in Table 5–25.[26]

25 The total debt rose to 578 million Mexican pesos, or 289 million dollars.

26 The sum into which the debt was converted after the Dublan conversion was considerably reduced. See Table 5–25.

TABLE 5–26 EXPORTS
(*in millions of Mexican pesos*)

1884	47.0
1893	93.4
1900	160.0
1910	281.2

SOURCE: *Estadísticas Económicas del Porfiriato,* p. 75.

TABLE 5–27 ENGLISH AND UNITED STATES CAPITAL INVESTED IN MEXICO
(*in millions of dollars*)

	1883	1902	1911
United States	30.0	501.6	1,057.1
Great Britain	163.5 (1880)	327.0 (1900)	437.5 (1910)
Total of Both	193.5	828.6	1,494.6

SOURCE: D'Olwer, "Las Inversiones Extranjeras," pp. 1132–1135, 1140 (the figure for Great Britain is in pounds; the conversion was effected by the author). Cited in Tables 5–14, 5–15, 5–16.

The evolution of exports is indicated in Table 5–26.

As is evident, the foreign debt showed a marked increase at the beginning of the period. From 51 million dollars in 1850 it increased to 116.5 million in 1888. With the conversion of that same year, it was reduced to 73 million, and then in 1893 it was increased to 95.5 million, where it was maintained with only slight increases until 1905, when sizable amounts of bonds were emitted to purchase the railroads. In any event, its growth is less than that of exports, which should signify a lighter burden on the economy as a whole. But direct capital investment had the greatest proportionate growth and resulted in a significant outflow of capital because of the remission of profits abroad. By observing the evolution of British and United States capital, shown in Table 5–27, which constituted the majority of foreign capital invested at

TABLE 5–28 PROFIT RETURNS FROM ENGLISH AND NORTH AMERICAN CAPITAL (*in millions of dollars*)

1883	1902	1911
11.6	49.7	89.7

SOURCE: The estimates of the author based on data from Table 5–27.

TABLE 5–29 ANNUAL AMOUNT OF INTEREST ON THE FOREIGN DEBT (*in millions of dollars*)

1888	1900	1910
7.0	5.8	6.0

SOURCE: The author's evaluation based on data in Table 5–25 and on the following rates of nominal interest, found in Turlington, *Mexico and Her Foreign Creditors,* p. 345.

Year	Nominal	Real
1888	6	8.01
1890	6	6.95
1893	6	9.87
1899 (conversion)	5	5.32
1904	4	4.71
1910 (conversion)	4	4.41

that moment, it may be noted that their combined rate of growth exceeded even that of exports and that the remission of profits abroad must have been an important burden on the Mexican balance of payments.

If we calculate that those capital investments yielded a minimum profit of 6 percent for these years, the outflow in concept of profits must have been those shown in Table 5–28.

On the other hand, the amount of interest payments on the foreign debt was much lower, as suggested in Table 5–29.

TABLE 5–30 PROFIT RETURNS AND INTEREST FROM THE DEBT IN RELATION TO EXPORTS
(*in millions of dollars*)

	Exports of Gold and Metals Prices	Profit Return	Interest on Debt
1883–1884	40.3	11.16	7.0
1902–1903	85.2	49.7	5.8
1910–1911	140.0	89.7	6.0

SOURCE: See Tables 5–28 and 5–29. *Estadísticas Económicas del Porfiriato,* pp. 75 and 152.

The significance of both categories in terms of total exports can be seen in Table 5–30.

It appears, therefore, that the foreign debt did not weigh so heavily as direct investments on the instability of the foreign sector. On the contrary, in some measure the debt served as an initial factor in attracting capital investments which, though proportionately minor at the beginning of the period of growth, amply exceeded the amount invested in government bonds by the end of the period.

6

ARGENTINA: AGRICULTURAL EXPORTS

Although independence in the rest of Spanish America was followed by a decline in production and trade from loss of markets, a rupture in trade routes, depredation, and wars, this did not occur in the Río de la Plata, which in the eighteenth century had begun exporting hides and other cattle by-products from its coastal hinterland. Before finding an outlet through exportation, which was limited because of legal and practical restrictions, the earliest agrarian and cattle production from the Río de la Plata coastal area was directed toward the north (Potosí), as was the whole economic life of the country at that time. Thousands of mules traveled from the coast along the road to Upper Peru to the fair in Lerma and then on to Potosí; these beasts of burden were to be used in the mines as a replacement for diminishing Indian Labor.[1] The Río de la Plata and Venezuela,[2] areas neglected in the early

1 They came principally from Santa Fe, Entre Ríos, and la Banda Oriental. See Tulio Halperin-Donghi, "El Río de la Plata al comenzar el siglo XIX," *Ensayos de Historia Social* (Buenos Aires: Facultad de Filosofía y Letras, University of Buenos Aires, 1961); and Halperin-Donghi, *The Aftermath of Revolution in Latin America.* The mule trade marks the beginning of cattle raising in the Río de la Plata. See Horacio Giberti, *Historia económica de la ganadería argentina* (Buenos Aires: Raigal, 1954). The decline in the Indian population seems to be a general phenomenon throughout the Spanish American empire, though precise data regarding the Peruvian viceroyalty are lacking. See David Noble Cook, "La población indígena en Perú colonial" in *América colonial, población y economía,* Anuario 6 del Instituto de Investigaciones Históricas, (Rosario; Universidad del Litoral, 1965). In Peru a scarce supply of labor was further aggravated by the problem of a large number of wandering Indians.

2 For Venezuela's shift toward Atlantic overseas trade, see Tulio Halperin-Donghi, *Historia contemporánea de América Latina* (Madrid: Alianza, 1969), p. 28; and Halperin-Donghi, *The Aftermath of Revolution.*

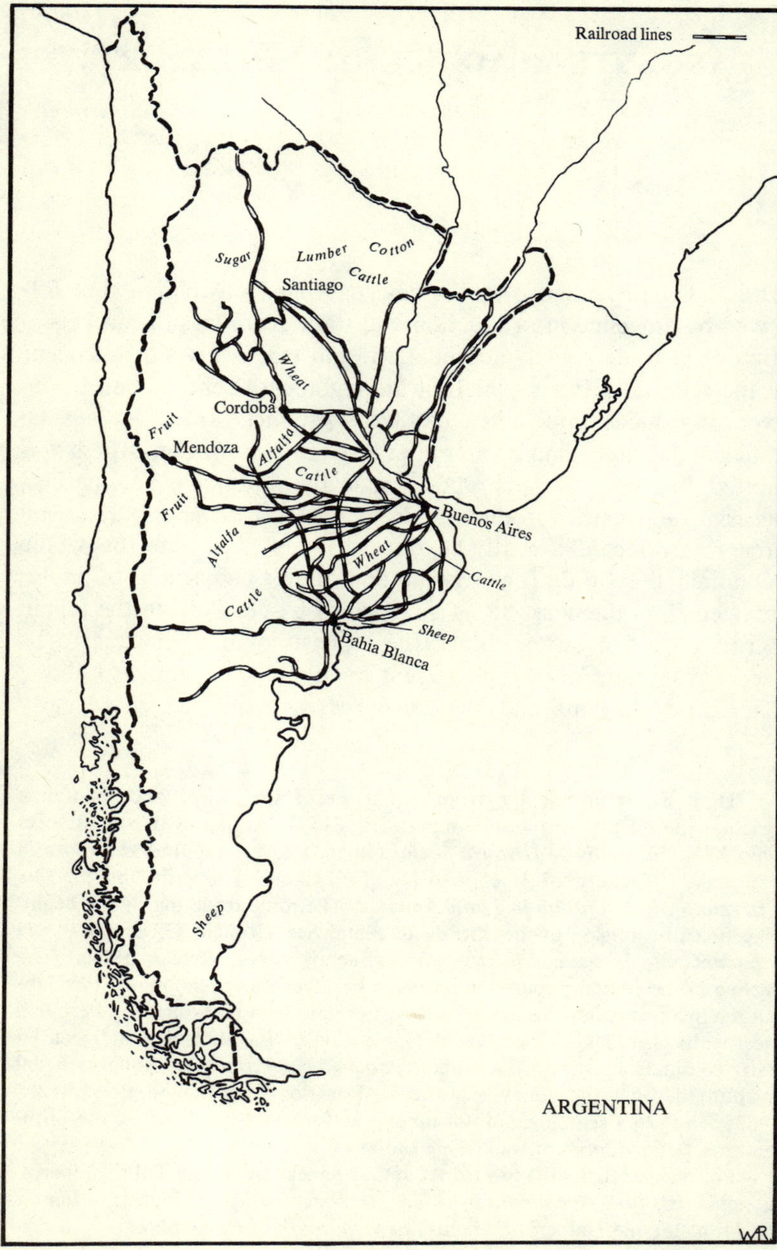

WILLOW ROBERTS

centuries of colonization, were the ones that best adjusted to the new conditions of world trade in the nineteenth century.

While it is true that the export of cattle products (hides) provided the Río de la Plata with an alternative to the exploitation of minerals, the old staple of the Spanish American economy, at a time when the old colonial political structures were disintegrating, this did not occur in those countries which had formerly been the most advanced regions in the vast Spanish empire in America—Mexico and Peru. They, instead, experienced a prolonged period of prostration in the years following the independence movement. It cannot be claimed, however, that the Río de la Plata passed through this period free from problems. There were some immediate ones, such as financial impoverishment, which persisted for a long time as a result of the loss of Potosí silver,[3] and others which lingered even longer. Mobilization for the war not only brought with it important consequences but also affected the social structure. The new orientation in production and trade resulted in a society that was more militarized and also more rural. While the urban crisis was extremely grave in some places, in others displaced commercial sectors sought better and more lucrative opportunities in rural areas. Though rural society was undoubtedly more *barbarous* in some ways, it was also more democratic.[4] Although the provinces of the Río de la Plata did not maintain a mobilized army beyond 1820 nor military operations within its

[3] When the Buenos Aires Junta of 1810 was proclaimed, the provincial court in Charcas resolved upon the incorporation of Upper Peru under the authority of the Peruvian viceroyalty. Conflicts and wars with the royalists continued until 1824 when the last battle of independence was fought in Ayacucho. Bolívar's Colombian army under orders from Marshal Sucre entered Upper Peru and a new nation, Bolivia, was formed. The provinces of Río de la Plata and then the province of Buenos Aires obtained monetary revenue (especially, in foreign currency, the pound sterling) through the export trade. Concerning the Río de la Plata's colonial evolution in the years following independence, see Juan Alvarez, "La evolución económica 1810–1829. Comercio, industria, moneda, ganaderia y agricultura," Academia Nacional de la Historia, in *Historia de la Nación Argentina desde sus orígenes hasta su organización definitiva en 1862,* vol. 7, director Ricardo Levene (Buenos Aires: El Ateneo, 1961–1962), part 1 of chap. 7.

[4] See Halperin-Donghi, *Historia contemporánea de América Latina,* pp. 137, 138.

territory after 1816, the war with Spain was extremely long in America and continued until 1824, and civil wars (in between the war with Brazil in 1826), which lasted until the 1840s, did, in fact, have the same effect. The military mobilization of society meant a drain on resources from the productive process in addition to depredation and loss of wealth. But prior to the national government's dissolution in 1820 significant growth had occurred. This began around the end of the century, with an important expansion of trade, stimulated by the imperial legislation on free trade, and it continued during the first decades of the nineteenth century.

This increase in exports is reflected in a no less significant population increase, as Table 6–1 indicates.

Expansion was linked to the reorientation of an economy which at first served as a source of supply (mules) for Upper Peru, then as an intermediary port which supplanted Lima, exchanging silver for manufactured goods, and finally was transformed into a monoproductive livestock zone (hides and to a lesser extent jerked meat and by-products for export). This occurred as a result of the appearance of markets which were lacking within the country itself. What was involved, therefore, was not the reallocation of production between domestic or external sectors, but rather the placement of a surplus for which there was no outlet in the domestic market. Abundant lands and a temperate climate made the area particularly suited to agriculture and cattle development that found no opportunity for commercializing (in any significant volumes) in the first two centuries of the colonial period. Not only the obstacles established by the Spanish crown for colonial trade, but also market demand and transportation conditions were hindrances to trade, until the nineteenth century. In spite of the liberal politics of the independent government, these obstacles persisted for a long time in the case of agricultural production. Without a nearby market for grain, such as the one Peru constituted for Chile, Buenos Aires was too far removed from centers of consumption (the Brazilian slave diet included jerked meat but not wheat) to permit the possibility of trading it abroad. And further, while cattle were self-transportable, wagon transport from production zones to urban centers, even when close by, was too costly to

TABLE 6–1 POPULATION OF BUENOS AIRES IN 1778, 1800, AND 1824

1778	50,000
1800	71,668
1824	163,216

SOURCE: Woodbine Parish, *Buenos Aires y las provincias del Río de la Plata* (Buenos Aires: Hachette, 1958), pp. 175, 176. Statistics from Buenos Aires Census of 1778, from Azara for 1800 and from the Official Register of the City of Buenos Aires for 1824.

allow domestic grain to compete with imported wheat.[5] This created a long delay until new circumstances of a technological nature made agricultural development in the Pampas area feasible.[6]

This reorientation of production affected the regional structure of what had been the most recently created viceroyalty. Once prosperous areas were relegated, while others, heretofore forgotten, were expanding. This was reflected not only in changes in the structure of the population, but also in the axis of the urban network,[7] which redirected itself from being oriented toward the North (Córdoba, Tucumán, Salta, Potosí) to facing the coastal-fluvial system (Paraná and Uruguay rivers and the Río de la Plata). Moreover, this may be noted particularly in the general ruralization of social environment. The population of the countryside grew in the first years of independence much more rapidly

5 It was many years later with the advent of peace in the central zones of Santa Fe bordering the Paraná, the only navigable river in the Argentine Pampas zone, that it was possible to develop a productive zone geared originally not to export, but to supplying domestic urban centers.

6 Concerning this, see Roberto Cortés Conde, "Algunos Rasgos de la Expansión Territorial en Argentina en la Segunda Mitad del Siglo XIX," in *Desarrollo Económico,* vol. 8, no. 29 (April–June 1968).

7 Roberto Cortés Conde, "Tendencias en el Crecimiento de la Población Urbana en la Argentina," *Actas del 38 Congreso de Americanistas* (Stuttgart, Germany, 1968).

TABLE 6–2 GROWTH OF THE PROVINCE OF BUENOS AIRES, CITY-COUNTRY RELATION

	Year	City	Country	Total
	1779	24,205	12,925	37,130
	1823	68,896	74,600	143,496
Annual Increase (percentage)	1779–1823	4.19	10.84	6.51

SOURCE: For 1779, Gregorio Ramos Mejía in *Revista del Plata,* No. 2, October 1823 and for 1823, *Registro Estadístico de la Provincia de Buenos Aires,* cited by Burgin, *Economic Aspects of Argentine Federalism,* p. 26.

than that of the city, as Table 6–2 indicates. It must be recalled that Spanish colonization had been predominantly urban.

The changes in the orientation of production had diverse consequences on the development of Argentine regions. Deprived of the Upper Peruvian market, northern and central Argentina found no substitute on the coast, which, while marketing its primary production abroad, was receiving manufactured goods in exchange. The latter more than replaced (and at a lower price) colonial artisan production. Lacking a substitute market this area did not possess adequate conditions for adjusting its production to the new structure of commerce. The northeastern (Litoral) provinces, with conditions similar to those of Buenos Aires, had only one obstacle to foreign trade, the restriction on navigation of inland rivers imposed on foreign flags. According to Burgin, if the Revolution was excessive for the interior, it was not enough for the Litoral area.[8]

Buenos Aires's development, which by 1820 was considerable, was limited during the next two decades, though much less so than the other Argentine provinces, by the cost of wars which persisted into the forties. At that time a strong governor in the province of Buenos Aires imposed order that assured an age of prosperity.[9] Nevertheless, at that point Buenos Aires lacked possibilities for expansion, which it later found in wool. In 1848, toward the end

8 Miron Burgin, *The Economic Aspects of Argentine Federalism* (Cambridge, Mass.: Harvard University Press, 1946), p. 122.

9 Halperin-Donghi, *Historia contemporánea de América Latina,* p. 203.

TABLE 6–3 SOME ARGENTINE ITEMS OF EXPORT BETWEEN 1822 AND 1850 (*in gold pesos*)

	Skins and Hides	Wool	Tallow	Grain	Meat and Animals	Total Exports
1829	3,516,040	30,334	65,271	—	329,638	5,200,000
1837	3,473,056	329,412	150,373	70,793	446,192	5,637,138
1848	2,918,475	681,800	1,213,460	—	418,870	5,458,020
1850	6,428,490	755,000	1,045,150	—	781,460	9,917,565

SOURCE: Parish, *Buenos Aires y las Provincias,* pp. 511, 512. (Amounts for 1848 and 1850 are given in pounds sterling. The conversion, 1 pound=5 silver pesos, is the author's. The figures for 1848 are those of the second half of that year.)

of the Rosas period, exports remained at the level of the 1820s. Only in 1850, nearly the dawn of the Urquiza uprising, did foreign trade enter a new period of expansion.[10]

Relative stagnation was manifest in another manner: the fall in the rate of growth of the population, which from 1820 to 1850 was below the levels reached in the second decade of the nineteenth century. This is shown in Table 6–4.

10 One could say that the isolationist, unprogressive attitude of the governor of Buenos Aires in not promoting immigration and settlement and cultivation of new lands affected this. Cf. Carlos Díaz Alejandro, *Essays on the Economic History of the Argentine Republic* (New Haven, Conn.: Yale University Press, 1970).

It is even less probable that this opposition to colonization expressed the interests of Buenos Aires landholders (as has often been claimed). Nothing indicates that the landholders would have opposed any progress of which, as was later shown, they would be if not the only, certainly not the least, beneficiaries. What probably occurred, and this differentiates Argentine development from that of the North American countries, was first, a long period of conflicts and political upheavals. And then—and this is equally important—Argentina's geographic location at the extreme south of America.

It must have seemed impossible in the 1840s to assure a powerful migratory influx to match that of the United States. Also, Argentina, prior to the development of railroads, did not have North America's advantage in a transportation system, that is, the canals, which stimulated the first territorial expansion. Regarding this, see also Robert W. Fogel, *Railroads and American Economic Growth* (Baltimore, Md.: Johns Hopkins Press, 1964).

TABLE 6–4 POPULATION GROWTH OF THE ARGENTINE REPUBLIC

Decades	Growth per Thousand Inhabitants per Decade
1809–1819	30
1819–1829	20
1829–1839	21
1839–1849	22
1849–1859	39
1859–1869	33

SOURCE: Argentine Republic, *Primer Censo de la República Argentina, 1869* (Buenos Aires, Imprenta del Porvenir, 1872), p. xx.

In the second half of the century European industry demanded raw materials. Not only the trade in cotton but also that of wool were areas of expansion in the textile industry. The addition of wool to the export of hides resulted in an important increase in overall exports, as Table 6–5 indicates.

Sheep raising, which needed the best lands, required a larger proportion of labor (though much less than did agriculture) than did cattle raising geared toward hide production. The first population movements, though timid and limited, occurred when sheep raising expanded. It was, however, agriculture which produced the most important changes in the structure of Argentina's economy and society, as well as an expansive process of unusual dimensions.[11]

Agricultural development was postponed for over half a century, not so much as a result of a presumed unhealthy resistance from cattle-raising landowners, but rather from other diverse causes. One cause was the distance from foreign (European) markets. Once a certain international specialization of labor was determined, and industrialized countries began importing grain, they did so from the most backward areas of Europe itself. Then the European market was entered by countries with the best and

[11] On the agrarian expansion see James R. Scobie, *Revolution on the Pampas* (Austin, Tex.: University of Texas Press, 1964).

TABLE 6–5 MAIN EXPORTS FROM ARGENTINA TO GREAT BRITAIN BETWEEN 1850–1854 AND 1870–1874
(*in millions of pounds sterling*)

Years	**Total Exports**	**Hides and Skins**	**Wool**	**Tallow**	**Grains and Flax**	**Meat and Animals**
1854	1,285	448	107	415	—	—
1858–1862	6,562	2,849	985	1,261	—	—
1863–1867	5,425	2,071	1,060	1,125	—	—
1870–1874	9,253	3,898	1,181	2,941	—	—

SOURCE: H. S. Ferns, *Britain and Argentina in the Nineteenth Century* (New York: Oxford University Press, 1960), p. 494. Calculated from *Parliamentary Papers,* cited in H. S. Ferns, "Investment and Trade Between Britain and Argentina in the Nineteenth Century," *Economic History Review,* 2d series, vol. 3, no. 2 (1960).

most frequent maritime communications (the United States, for example). Another cause was the narrowness of the local market in a sparsely populated country. But, furthermore, the domestic market suffered from the cost of land transportation to potential markets, the urban centers, plus the lack of navigable rivers in the Pampas region,[12] thus making those centers inaccessible to the agricultural production of the Pampas.[13]

Extensive cattle raising was the appropriate response to the relative supply of factors which existed until almost the end of the nineteenth century. Its exploitation did not require (nor could it obtain) the incorporation of factors then scarce in the Río de la Plata—labor and capital. The development of this export industry did not demand foreign factors. But this production pattern, a result of the relative supply of factors, contributed to maintaining unchanged the structure to which it responded. Since the production of cowhides required very little labor, some of it seasonal, the Pampas area persisted in a chronic demographic poverty, with few urban settlements aside from the ports. For the same reason the

[12] The exceptions were the Paraná and, to some degree, Uruguay. When Santa Fe was pacified and the population extended to the Paraná, the first attempts in agricultural development occurred.

[13] See the example cited for corn in Chivilcoy. Thomas J. Hutchinson, *Buenos Aires y Otras Provincias Argentinas* (Buenos Aires: Huarpes, 1945), p. 95.

distribution of income was extremely unequal, not because the rural peons received low salaries (they were, as is known, relatively high in relation to those paid in other parts of the world), but because income distribution corresponded to the production function in cattle raising for hides: it required little labor and was highly land-intensive.

If the results are analyzed in terms of population and distribution of income, it is evident that this type of production could not emerge from an extremely limited demand and an almost nonexistent national market. As for domestic activities which this activity might promote, its demands for inputs were almost nonexistent and, hence, practically nil in terms of backward linkages. As for forward linkages, they produced one substantial consequence, the growth of the meat-salting industry, which continued until nearly the beginning of this century. Corresponding also to this demographic conformation and economic organization was a hierarchical social structure, composed of two numerically sparse extremes and the almost total absence of the intermediary strata that had been more numerous in the more urbanized colonial life.[14] Though there were enormous differences between the two extremes in terms of power and wealth in land, their customs and austere life were extremely similar. Only the urban classes, with decreased economic power, would clash against this new barbarism.

The economic evolution of the entire first half of the century was limited by the technological characteristics of the export industry which emerged in the Río de la Plata. And this industry developed these characteristics instead of others due to the original conditions of its resources, their degree of technological evolution, and market conditions at the time.

Agriculture at the end of the nineteenth century, however, assumed and required a substantial modification in the assignation of resources, a more intensive use of labor. Its consequences on the economy and society as a whole likewise differed. Despite the fact that both agriculture and cattle raising are based on export

[14] José Luis Moreno, "La estructura social y demográfica de la Ciudad de Buenos Aires en el año 1778" in *América colonial población y economía,* Anuario 6 del Instituto de Investigaciones Históricas (Rosario: Universidad del Litoral, 1965).

(misleading many into referring to only one stage of Argentine export), there are substantial differences. The results of their later evolution were also different.[15]

The feature that distinguishes agriculture from the rawhide industry, and it is a fundamental one, is agriculture's greater use of labor. The need for a high degree of labor presumes additional requirements of food, transportation, construction, services, and the formation of urban communities. And further, especially for wheat, it supposes markets whose income levels are not excessively low and, finally, a transportation system that makes actual exploitation possible at a low cost. The confluence of all these factors produced profound changes in the structure of the Argentine economy and in the organization of production. Deriving also from the fact that there was a more labor-intensive production function, the distribution of income was more widespread.[16]

One of the most important backward linkages in this stage was the establishment of an important railroad network. Another result, a forward linkage and no less negligible, was the establishment of domestic resident industries for the processing of raw materials—mills, meat-packing plants, food products industries—which were geared not only to the foreign market, but to the domestic as well. The rise in the employment level had supple-

[15] Meat production is included along with agriculture, for it was a result of agricultural expansion.

[16] This applies even when salaries are lower, which actually occurred. This, furthermore, is in Argentina independent of the tenancy pattern. While North considers a tenancy structure based on the diffusion of family property as a condition for the dynamic effects of expanding primary activity (See Douglas North, "Agriculture in Regional Economic Growth," *Journal of Farm Economics,* vol. 41, no. 5 [December 1959]), this did not occur: the tenancy structure in 1914 was characterized by the fact that about 70 percent of the agricultural cattle-raising enterprise was operated by nonowners. Had there existed a larger number of landowners, the income would probably have been more equally distributed but essentially the following occurs: 1. A change is produced between the old pattern of extensive cattle ranching and the new agricultural pattern in the proportion of income received by labor. (See Roberto Cortés Conde, *"El Sector agricolo en el desarrollo económico argentino 1880–1910"* (Buenos Aires: ITDT, 1969). 2. The share of income received by labor is not high, but is received in cash. 3. The tenant is not bound to a self-sufficient unit (like the hacienda or the sugar plantation).

TABLE 6–6 COMPOSITION OF ARGENTINE IMPORTS
(*in percentages*)

Year	Food	Beverages	Textiles and Clothes	Raw Material and Manufactured Goods	Total
1876	28.0	17	25.5	29.5	100
1887	15.5	13	25.5	46.0	100
1896	16.0	8	34.0	42.0	100
1911	9.5	4	19.0	67.5	100

SOURCES: For 1876, *Estadística del comercio exterior y de la navegación interior y exterior correspondiente a 1880* (Buenos Aires, 1881), p. 37. For 1887 and 1896, *Anuario de la Dirección General de Estadística correspondiente a 1896* (Buenos Aires, 1897), p. 5. For 1911, *Anuario de la Dirección General de Estadística correspondiente a 1911* (Buenos Aires, 1912).

mentary effects in expanding demand. In order to supply domestic demand, resident activities sprang up, enjoying the advantages of location for the supply of raw materials. Food and beverages were among these, and they later extended to include textiles. The appearance of new resident industries was soon reflected in an import substitution process observable in the decline of certain import categories (food, beverages, and even textiles), whereas others (raw materials) increased. This is shown in Table 6–6.

Before considering the characteristics of the evolution of this process and its consequences, the factors contributing to its development may be examined.

EXOGENOUS FACTORS OF GROWTH

With the establishment of a sort of inter-European division of labor between countries in varying stages of development, the demand for grain in the Western European market opened around the middle of the century and at first was satisfied by Eastern Europe. Later, the United States and India joined the international market of grain, thereby producing a perceptible decline of prices. Navigation by way of the South Atlantic was still costly, and, furthermore, the possibility of finding markets that would sustain steady traffic was extremely limited (considering the volume required in shipping grain). The opportunity to transport immigrants during a certain period with their passage paid for by governmental agencies provided an incentive to shipping firms that, although able to take on grain in the Río de la Plata, had not the assurance of the same proportion of cargo when returning there.[17] Reduced freightage, which made the export of grain profitable over such long distances, was one important factor for shipping companies, while complete cargoes in trips both to and from Europe was another equally important factor. For a long time immigrants served as a counterpart to grain for this purpose. More than the European demand for grain, the modifications in the transportation system and trade routes, as well as a series of governmental decisions (like immigration laws and others, which will be discussed presently), brought the production of the Pampas closer to European markets.

There is no doubt that movements of capital and labor were the other two important exogenous factors in this pattern of growth through trade which not only required the use of a given factor, land, but also the incorporation of other external and at that time scarce factors—labor and capital. These external, nonresident factors were mobilized through circumstances stemming from their place of origin: their existence in a state of abundance signified that they could obtain higher returns in areas where they were scarce. However, the sole difference in incomes or return is not enough if the receiving country fails to provide the suitable conditions for their settling in the country. These general conditions correspond to different mechanisms which will be designated here as endogenous factors of growth.

Endogenous Factors of Growth

The following will be discussed, though not exhaustively, on various analytical levels: (1) population policy, (2) investment policy, (3) monetary and export policy, and (4) establishment of an institutional structure. Although all of these factors are intimately connected, they are not linked by a causal sequence (no

[17] See Douglas North, "Ocean Freight Rates," *Journal of Economic History*, no. 18 (1958).

single one is merely a cause or consequence of the other). For analytical purposes, however, each will be treated separately.

POPULATION POLICY

The need to obtain cheap labor in a country suffering chronically from sparseness of population which could not be modified merely by its vegetative growth[18] by means of incorporating a foreign adult population was widely endorsed by people of the times, who were conscious of the most recent North American experiment. The government dating from the Confederation period played an extremely active role in promoting immigration, which it regarded as a panacea for many of the evils which beset the new nation. The establishment of colonies, the payment of lodging and in certain instances of transportation expenses, and the publicity about benefits offered by Argentina (though disproportionate in the promise of land, accurate insofar as the conditions of life and work, which were undoubtedly an improvement over those in the countries of the immigrants' origin)[19] were contributing factors in promoting the influx of immigrants.

Although the policy designed to obtain a selective immigration failed, since most of the new arrivals apparently did not possess specific qualifications or incorporate more capital (which would have meant immediate capitalization for the country), the policy, nonetheless, was not frustrated insofar as a significant mass of people were incorporated into the active population and worked on a hitherto unused resource. The beginning of production in substantial volume of a resource hitherto only meagerly exploited (the land) was translated immediately into a rapid increase in wealth.[20] The incorporation of immigrants was possible because

[18] M. G. and E. T. Mulhall, *Handbook of the River Plate* (Buenos Aires: Standard Court, 1892).

[19] Emilio Lahitte, *Informes y estudios de la división de estadísticas y economía rural* (Buenos Aires: Talleres gráficos de la oficina meteorológica, 1908), p. 65.

[20] Proponents of the immigration policy sought, in general, immigrants from northern European zones, who were regarded as better workers. This commonly held belief was disputed by British consuls:

> It is owing to the Englishman's innate aversion to all change that he has not generally been a success in this country as a labourer, and it is for this reason

TABLE 6–7 NET IMMIGRATION 1857–1900

Years	Total Immigration	Emigration	Net Immigration
1857–1860	20,000	8,900	11,100
1861–1870	159,570	82,976	76,594
1871–1880	260,885	175,763	85,122
1881–1890	841,122	202,455	637,667
1891–1900	648,326	328,444	319,882

SOURCE: Gustavo Beyhaut et al., *Inmigración y desarrollo económico* (Buenos Aires: Department of Sociology, 1961). Calculated with figures from *Resúmen estadístico de movimiento inmigratorio,* Dirección General de Inmigración.

of political stability which was finally attained after 1865 and by the spread of railways.

Nevertheless, for agricultural development this growth in immigration did not suffice. The fact that this process was accompanied by an active investment policy in the infrastructure meant that a great mass of newly arrived workers was absorbed by the urban sector. The latter (which offered more immediate expansion and less risk) thus competed with the agricultural sector for the scarce labor supply during the first decade of the expansion policy which began in the 1880s. It was the crisis of 1890 which, by

chiefly that he competes unfavourably with many other foreign labourers who, through their thriftiness and the ease with which they adopt their new life, are far more successful. British immigrants expect far too much on arrival here, and their would-be employers expect harder work of them than they are usually willing to give. Hence the bad name they have out in this country. Given workmen of several nationalities, such as British, Italian, German, and French, all equally good, employers of labour here would at once put aside the British workman, and take any one of the other foreigners, and by preference the Italian. The foreigner works harder than the Englishman, is more amenable, and does not get drunk. Even British employers of labour infinitely prefer foreign to British labour for these reasons.

Cf. Consular Reports, 1893. This flow of migrants which in certain places occurred at particular periods and then halted was expressly discouraged in some instances (England). Quoted in Oscar Cornblit, "Inmigrantes y Empresarios de la Política Argentina" in *Los Fragmentos del Poder* (Buenos Aires: Alvarez, 1969).

detaining the investment process,[21] left a considerable mass of labor free, permitting a rapid expansion of the cultivated area in the years that followed.

However, not only was there a labor supply released by the urban sector. One must not omit the labor stemming from secondary and particularly tertiary sectors in the interior (not because of any high degree of development, but precisely for the opposite reason: the fact that a traditional textile sector on the one hand and activities related to older means of transportation which had engaged a large number of people on the other hand, both declined). As those activities were replaced by more modern ones, a significant quantity of manpower was freed.[22]

Aside from the crisis of 1890, which had a pronounced effect in the last decade of the century in reducing the cost of land and labor, an agricultural procedure, well known from antiquity, spread and attained notable dimensions in Argentina. This was the leasing of land which, among other things, provided a source of labor without the need for significant investment, as the landowners could retain ownership of the land while small parcels were leased to farmers. This permitted the owners of large landholdings simultaneously to continue to raise cattle and to have some areas of their land brought into cultivation under the system of tenancy (sharecropping, renting for cash, and so forth). This system was different from the previously existing patterns of private ownership in agricultural development (as was the case earlier in the Santa Fe colonies). The fact that a great number of landholders began to

[21] The hypothesis that the rural sector in 1890 provided a safety valve for urban overemployment when the crisis of 1890 halted the strong wave of foreign investments and imports was developed by the author. See Roberto Cortés Conde, "Patrones de asentamiento y explotación agropecuario en los nuevos territorios argentinos (1890–1910)" in *Tierras nuevas, expansión territorial y ocupación del suelo en América* (*Siglos XVI–XIX*) ed., Alvaro Jara (Mexico City: El Colegio de México, 1969). Between 1888 and 1890 the area under cultivation rose by 22 percent while immigration balances declined. Exports thereby increased. (See Tables 6–20 and 6–21 of the text.)

[22] Gabriel Carrasco in his prefatory comments to the second volume of the *Segundo Censo Naciónal,* vol. 2, p. CXLIV, says, "Drivers, herders, muleteers, etc., who in 1869 numbered 7,845, have been reduced to 4,619, being advantageously replaced by the 4,824 RR employees who did not exist at the time of the first census."

TABLE 6–8 PROFESSIONS WHICH DIMINISHED BETWEEN 1869 AND 1895

Professions	1869	1895
Weavers	94,032	39,380
Muleteers, Cattle Drivers, etc.	7,845	4,619

SOURCE: Argentina, *Segundo Censo de la República Argentina,* 1895 (Buenos Aires: Talleres Tipográficos de la Penitenciaria Nacional, 1898).

raise crops under this system can be explained by the failure of speculative expectations which had activated the land market in the five-year period preceding the crisis of 1890. In view of the unlikelihood of obtaining any considerable capital gains through a rapid spectacular rise in land values, the leasing of land provided the landowner with at least some rent.

For the tenants in a period of declining land prices, leasing seemed preferable to buying and burdening oneself with a mortgage that had to be paid in the future when the land prices would be less than present ones. And given that grain prices in the early 1890s were actually on the rise whereas those of land were declining, the amount paid for rent was a decreasing function of income obtained from the sale of their products.[23]

These circumstances may possibly explain why at the onset of a period of agricultural expansion (after 1890), marked by a declining trend in land prices, agriculturists did not buy land but worked it as tenants. The fact that proprietors were reluctant to sell offers a valid though inadequate explanation. Had there existed a strong interest on behalf of farmers for existing property, given the depressive trend of the land market and the landowners' need for income, those lands would have been obtainable on the market.[24] On the other hand, with the system of land rents landowners were

[23] Those who preferred the tenant system whereby the owner remained linked to the producer's enterprises undoubtedly realized this.

[24] See Roberto Cortés Conde, "El Mercado de Tierras en Argentina," 6th Congreso de Americanistas (Rome, 1972). However, it seems that the value of land offered for sale was greater than what has been estimated (Buenos Aires: ITDT, 1972).

not forced to abandon all of their property, but only portions of it and generally small ones, which they put under cultivation. Nor can a valid explanation be found in the dependence on alfalfa in the feeding of high-grade cattle raised for meat export, a phenomenon which appeared at least a decade later. The cultivation of alfalfa began in the areas of settlements in the provinces of Santa Fe and Córdoba on the Central Argentino railroad route as an agricultural exploitation destined for the market and not for cattle feed.

On the other hand, the second period of agricultural expansion that occurred in the first decade of the twentieth century, particularly after 1905, is related to the growth of the cattle industry, alfalfa production, and other combined crops. Leasing then became even more widespread. How can this be explained? What occurred then, unlike the events of the 1890s, was that although the producer's profits were rising, land prices rose even more. The producer's profit always lagged behind (and at a very great distance) the evolution of land values. Hence, despite the producer's growing earnings, he was paradoxically increasingly unable to purchase land. (Precisely the reverse of what occurred in the preceding period.)

One fact that must be indicated in relation to both periods is that during the 1890s the most prevalent form of leasing was sharecropping, whereas in the twentieth century the most common form of leasing was of payment in cash. The proprietor sought thereby a more favorable position. In the 1890s, when grain prices were rising, it was best to participate in the producer's profit; but in the next decade it was preferable to fix the rent in relation to land value, which was increasing steadily.

An explanation is given for this phenomenon of an impressive increase of land values, that is believed to lie in the limited supply of agricultural land (which was assumed to be unlimited or at least much greater than it was), in the rapid increase of land under cultivation (several million hectares within a few years), and also in the continued flow of immigrants who had an important effect on the demand for land (whether it was for purchase or otherwise).[25]

[25] A detailed explanation may be found in ibid.

TABLE 6–9 CULTIVATED AREA, 1895–1914

Years	**Surface (in thousand of hectares)**	**Years**	**Surface (in thousand of hectares)**
1895	4,892	1905	13,801
1896	5,570	1906	13,898
1897	5,372	1907	14,612
1898	5,983	1908	15,831
1899	6,427	1909	18,776
1900	7,311	1910	20,367
1901	7,638	1911	21,839
1902	9,115	1912	22,988
1903	10,685	1913	24,092
1904	11,424	1914	24,317

Increase per Five-Year Period

Period	*Percentage*
1895–1899	6.26
1900–1904	7.78
1905–1909	7.20
1909–1914	3.80

SOURCE: *Estadísticas Agrícolas* (Buenos Aires: Ministerio de Agricultura, *Dirección de económia rural y estadística, 1905–1914*).

The expansion of areas under cultivation which reflects the impressive growth in the Argentine economy was a function of the new availability of land arising from the construction of railroad lines and of the incorporation of a labor force. Around 1914 it had, however, almost reached its maximum extension (the greatest extension reached for all times was 28 million hectares).

INVESTMENT POLICY: The Role of the State

What remains to be seen is if modernization of the productive structure, a prerequisite for embarking on agricultural development, resulted solely from the action of market forces or if this was not sufficient and its advancement therefore required either

TABLE 6–10 DISTRIBUTION OF EXPENSES IN ACCORDANCE WITH NATIONAL BUDGETS FOR 1894 AND 1895
(*in percentages*)

	1894	**1895**
Salaries and Other Administrative Expenses	32.8	34.6
Investments in Developmental Works	11.1	7.1
Public Debt	40.3	43.6
Others	15.8	14.7
Total	100.0	100.0

SOURCE: *Memorias del Ministerio de Hacienda de la Nación* (Buenos Aires, 1894–1895).

direct or indirect government action. In order to assess the degree to which the government participated in the process of establishing infrastructural capital, the proportion allotted in the national budget for that expense must be ascertained.[26] The two years 1894 and 1895 are taken as an example because they fell neither at the peak of the expansive process of the 1880s nor during the more depressed years following the crisis of 1891–1892.

According to Table 6–10 the amount spent on investments basic for development appears extremely small in relation to the total expense. However, this seems rather distorted because of the high proportion allotted to payment of the public debt. Why, for what purposes, was that debt contracted? To determine this, we have examined the composition of the debt in relation to the ends toward which these funds were employed by those who contracted them. This is shown in Table 6–11.

It is thus evident that the portion of the public debt allocated to works of infrastructure was relatively high.[27]

Returning to the budget breakdown for the year 1894, if the

[26] For this, the sectors included in it must be recategorized according to the ends sought.

[27] On this point the author differs with the criteria of Wilkie, who, when studying the case of Mexico, classified the entire public debt as an administrative expense. See James Wilkie, *The Mexican Revolution* (Berkeley and Los Angeles, Calif.: University of California Press, 1967).

TABLE 6–11 COMPOSITION OF ARGENTINA'S PUBLIC DEBT, 1824–1913
(*in percentages of the total*)

	1824	1894	1897	1902	1906	1913
Investments in Infrastructure	51.5	63.0	66.0	50.0	56.0	53.5
Railroads	22.0	16.0	26.5	23.0	26.0	26.0
Others (Ports, Telegraph Lines, Sanitary Facilities, Public Works)	29.5	47.0	39.5	27.0	30.0	27.5
Other Investments	6.5	8.5	7.0	5.0	5.0	9.5
Finances	42.0	28.5	27.0	45.0	39.0	37.0

SOURCES: Elaboration by the author of material compiled from *The Argentine Year Book,* 1902, 1914, 1915–1916 and E. Tornquist and Co., *The Economic Development of the Argentine Republic* (Buenos Aires, 1919).

TABLE 6–12 TOTAL INVESTMENTS IN INFRASTRUCTURE IN THE 1894 BUDGET

Public Debt in the Budget	40.3	
Investments in Infrastructure in the Public Debt	63.1	
Investments in Infrastructure in the Public Debt as a Percentage of the Total Budget		23.5
Proportion of the Budget Designed for Infrastructural Investment		11.1
Total Investments in Infrastructure in the Budget		36.6

SOURCES: See Tables 6–10 and 6–11.

portion within the public debt corresponding to investments in infrastructure is separated and to it is added the amount allocated in the budget, it may be seen that the total spent on infrastructure works comes to 36.6 percent of the general total, as Table 6–12 shows.

During that same period, where was foreign capital investment

TABLE 6–13 COMPOSITION OF FOREIGN CAPITAL INVESTED IN ARGENTINA IN 1892
(*in percentage of the total*)

Investments in Bonds of the Public Debt	44.6	
In Railroad Guarantees	26.2	
Total Invested with a Guarantee from the State or in State Bonds		70.8
Nonguaranteed Railroads	11.2	
Commercial and Industrial Companies	6.0	
Mortgage Documents	12.0	
Total Invested in the Private Sector, without State Intervention		29.2
		100.0

SOURCE: *Exposición sobre el estado económico y financiero de la Nación* (Buenos Aires: Ministerio de Hacienda, 1892), p. 149.

in the country primarily directed? From the report made by the minister of the treasury in 1892 on the economic and financial state of the nation, the estimate shown in Table 6–13 can be drawn up.

Suppliers of foreign capital were still not risking direct investments but preferred taking government bonds or putting money in firms that assured a safe return. The reaction of market strength, which later seemed so obvious, was not, in fact, that automatic and assumed slow and rather risky, although perhaps perceptible, returns. It was up to the government to take the first steps in providing basic infrastructure levels and enlarging the market. The policy of obtaining funds through public bonds was its principal instrument.

At a later date when the nation was pacified, works of infrastructure built, the population enlarged, and income had risen, there was a powerful flow of foreign investments, oriented toward direct investments which yielded more profitable returns. This is shown in Table 6–14.

As English capital represented more than two-thirds of the total of foreign investments, generally speaking it determined the overall

TABLE 6–14 INVESTMENTS OF FOREIGN CAPITAL IN ARGENTINA

Year	**Million of Pesos**
1892	836.8
1910	2,256.5
1911	2,752.1
1913	3,520.0

SOURCES: For 1892 estimates of the Ministerio de Hacienda in the Memorandum presented to Congress in 1892, cited by A. G. Ford, *El patrón oro, 1880–1914* (Buenos Aires: Editorial del Instituto, 1966), p. 154. The book was published in English by the Oxford University Press. For 1910, Schwenke's estimates in the *Review of the River Plate,* cited by Vernon Phelps, *International Economic Position of Argentina* (Philadelphia: University of Pennsylvania Press, 1938), p. 99. For 1911, Albert B. Martínez and Maurice Lewandowski, *The Argentine in the Twentieth Century,* trans. Bernard Miall (London: T. F. Unwin, 1911), pp. 352–353. For 1913, Bunge's estimates, taken from Phelps, *International Economic Position of Argentina.*

trend.[28] That being so, the composition of total foreign capital would follow that of English capital which is shown in Table 6–15 at its peak in 1908.

One could say that government action in directing this process of growth by specifically promoting, encouraging, or guaranteeing basic investments in infrastructure played a much more important role than is generally assumed and that the role of foreign capital, though quantitatively the most significant one, played a less active and risky role than is believed. If such is at all the case, the government must have exercised an entrepreneurial role despite the decidedly laissez faire convictions of those who figured prominently in the process of decision making and who had to seek

[28] In general, French and German capital had preferences different from those of British capital.

TABLE 6–15 COMPOSITION OF BRITISH INVESTMENT IN ARGENTINA IN 1908

Sectors	Percentages
Loans and Bonds	22.0
Railroads	57.0
Banks	3.0
Mortgages	2.5
Tramways	7.0
Electricity	2.0
Agriculture and Livestock	1.5
Mix	5.0
	100.0 (1,467,199.4 pesos)

SOURCE: Martínez and Lewandowski, *The Argentine in the Twentieth Century*.

more pragmatic responses to a situation which differed from that of other countries. Nevertheless, once the basic prerequisites—transportation means and market dimension—were attained, the government yielded to private enterprise. And it is not strange that at that point many firms preferred direct investments.

EXPORT AND MONETARY POLICY

The monetary policy was an important instrument in the action developed to enable Argentina to compete in the world market. Grain production for local consumption had begun in the Santa Fe area near the ports from which urban centers could be supplied. The area of settlements was extended with the construction of the Rosario-Bell Ville (Fraile Muerto) system of the Central Argentino Railway. Since the grain was originally destined for local consumption, however, little was ever exported.

Hides and wool continued until 1890 to rank as the most important export categories, since before that year the proportion of grains exported was very small.

Various obstacles prevented Argentine grain from reaching international grain markets:

1. Competition from the closer European market (with cheaper labor)

TABLE 6–16 COMPOSITION OF PRINCIPAL EXPORTS, BETWEEN 1875–1890
(*in percentages*)

Year	Hides and Skins	Wool	Tallow	Meat and Animals	Grains and Flax
1875	37.9	40.1	9.5	5.7	—
1880	36.1	42.9	3.9	6.5	0.9
1885	30.8	42.7	6.2	5.6	11.1
1890	23.4	35.5	3.3	7.9	26.9

SOURCE: Roberto Cortés Conde, Tulio Halperin-Donghi, and Haydée G. de Torres, *Evolución del Comercio Exterior Argentino* (Buenos Aires, 1966, mimeographed).

2. The lower cost of North American maritime transportation
3. With respect to land transportation, comparing the Argentine case with that of the United States, transportation to the ports was cheaper in Argentina once the railroad network had been established. This was not true before that, since while in the United States transportation was carried out by a network of canals—transportation by water was cheaper—in Argentina there was only the wagon, which was much more expensive.[29]
4. From 1885–1888 the speculative rise in land prices
5. The international declining price trend (intensified by incorporation of additional countries into the world supply)

Argentine production reached the international grain markets in significant proportions only after 1890. This was due not only to the discovery of fertile lands, but also to the removal of various obstacles which permitted that production to be placed on the market. In some cases this was the result of totally fortuitous situations. Crop failures in countries which had traditionally been a source of supply induced the search for other new sources.[30] Other situations, however, evolved from deliberate policy decisions

[29] References on this may be found in E. Lahitte, *Informes y estudios de la dirección de economía rural y estadística,* pp. 11 et seq.; for the U.S., Robert W. Fogel, *Railroads and American Economic Growth.*

[30] Alois C. Fliess, *La Producción Agrícola y Ganadera de la República Argentina en el año 1891* (Buenos Aires: Imprenta La Nación, 1892).

both foreign and domestic. Some happily coincided with profit for producers. North America's persistence in adhering to the gold standard provoked a rural crisis in the United States which indirectly favored the Argentine producer who benefited domestically from the flexible currency exchange which had been established in the country.[31] Involved also, as has been shown, were decisions of domestic policy relating to population, establishment of transportation networks, and so forth.

At this point those decisions having to do with monetary policy will be examined. The gold standard, which had been introduced in 1881, lasted until 1885. The interruption of the inflow of capital and the loan failure contributed to a crisis in the balance of payments, resulting in an outflow of gold which forced the authorities to decide for inconvertibility from 1885 to the end of the century.[32]

Though the causes which forced inconvertibility are clear, they do not explain why the system persisted until the end of the century, since the balance of trade had improved from 1890 onward. This undoubtedly was due to circumstances which were not acknowledged by their contemporaries. The effect in this instance was that earnings in the export sector obtained in gold (or in pounds sterling) were more valuable in terms of the domestic currency. Amid the sharp decline in international prices (due to increased supply) and given the obstacles hindering the placement of Argentine production in foreign markets, the gold premium was a strong incentive for producers.[33]

[31] This happened from 1885 to 1889 when Argentina had to go off the gold standard that it had adhered to in 1881. For the United States see Milton Friedman and Anna Jacobson Schwarts, *A Monetary History of the United States* (Princeton, N.J.: Princeton University Press, 1963).

[32] The narration may be found in John Williams, *Argentine International Trade under Inconvertible Paper Money* (Cambridge, Mass.: Harvard University Press, 1920).

[33] Matías Romero, *The Silver Standard in Mexico* (New York: The Knickerbocker Press, 1898), referring to the same situation already mentioned in Mexico says:

> The silver standard encourages very materially, so long as other leading commercial nations have the single gold standard, the increase of exports of domestic products, because the expenses of producing them, land, wages, rent, taxes, etc. are paid in silver and therefore their cost, as compared with their market value, is considerably less than that of similar articles produced or raised in single gold standard countries. When sold in gold markets,

By comparing the prices of grain in gold and in current pesos, as shown in Table 6–17, one can observe the extent to which the international trend of decreasing prices of grain was reversed.

This, of course, would produce benefits for the exporter as well as the farmer and cattle raiser who would receive their prices with the premium of gold value, providing that domestic prices rose less than did gold. That is, provided that the devaluation of the domestic purchasing power of the currency did not exceed its loss of value in international terms. Since indexes were lacking—and still are—on the cost of living or wholesale prices which could be used as deflators, it is only possible to make reasonable conjectures on

---

therefore, they bring very profitable prices, as they are converted into silver, at a high rate of exchange. These conditions have caused a great development in the exportation of some of our agricultural products, because they yield very large profits: coffee, for instance, which costs on an average about ten cents a pound to produce it, all expenses included, has been sold at about twenty cents in gold in foreign markets. The export of other agricultural products which did not pay when gold and silver were at par, that is, at the ratio of one to sixteen, is now remunerative, because there is returned to us in exchange more than we lose in the gold price of the article.

The same is the result of some agricultural products that we could not export before because their price in foreign markets was not remunerative. Such is the case, for instance, with beans, which at eight cents in gold make about sixteen cents in silver, it is a profitable price. Our exports for several years preceding 1869 were about,

a year	$20,000,000.00
1872–1873	$31,594,005.14
1888–1889	$60,158,423.02
1891–1892	$75,467,714.95
1892–1893	$87,509,207.00

The Statistical Bureau of the Mexican Government quotes the price of our exports in silver, and therefore to find them in gold they have to be reduced to the market price of silver, but, even reduced to one-half, the increase is very remarkable.

The silver standard is a great stimulus to the development of home manufactures, because foreign commodities have to be paid for in gold, and, owing to the high rate of exchange, their prices are so high that it pays well to manufacture some of them at home, our low wages also contributing to this result.

For these reasons we are increasing considerably our manufacturing plants, especially our cotton mills, smelters, etc., and we begin now to manufacture several articles that formerly we used to buy from foreign countries, and all this, notwithstanding that the mountainous character of our country, the want of interior navigable watercourses, and the scarcity of fuel, make manufacturing very expensive in Mexico.

TABLE 6–17 PRICE OF CEREALS, 1880–1903
(*in gold pesos, in pesos of national currency and in index numbers*)
(*base 1889:100*)

	Wheat (100 kg)		Corn (100 kg)		Mean Cereals		Mean Cereals (index numbers)	
Year	Gold	Pesos	Gold	Pesos	Gold	Pesos	Gold	Pesos
1880	7.22	7.22	2.25	2.25	4.735	4.735	195	108
1881	6.47	6.47	1.80	1.80	4.135	4.135	175	95
1882	5.36	5.36	2.03	2.03	3.695	3.695	152	85
1883	3.73	3.73	2.26	2.26	2.995	2.995	123	69
1884	3.99	3.99	1.86	1.86	2.925	2.925	121	67
1885	2.94	4.03	1.36	1.86	2.150	2.945	89	69
1886	4.24	5.90	1.76	2.45	3.000	4.170	124	96
1887	3.40	4.60	1.66	2.24	2.530	3.415	104	78
1888	2.70	4.00	2.03	3.00	2.365	3.500	97	80
1889	3.48[a]	6.27	1.37	2.46	2.425	4.365	100	100
1890	2.98	7.69	1.40	3.61	2.190	5.650	90	129
1891	3.64	13.61	2.40	8.97	3.020	11.295	124	259
1892	2.87	9.44	1.75	3.76	2.310	7.599	95	174
1893	2.37	7.68	1.96	6.35	2.165	7.014	89	161
1894	1.81	6.48	1.84	6.59	1.825	6.533	75	150
1895	2.09	7.19	1.34	4.61	1.715	5.899	71	185
1896	—	—	—	—	—	—	—	—
1897	3.56	10.36	1.16	3.57	2.360	6.867	97	157
1898	3.48	8.93	1.46	3.75	2.470	6.348	102	145
1899	2.40	5.40	1.23	2.77	1.815	4.084	75	94
1900	2.58	5.96	1.66	3.83	2.120	4.897	89	112
1901	2.80	6.50	1.92	4.45	2.360	5.475	97	125
1902	2.96	6.93	2.00	4.68	2.480	5.803	102	133
1903	2.79	6.33	1.81	4.11	2.300	5.221	95	120

[a] *Cortés Conde, Halperin-Donghi, and de Torres,* Evolución del Comercio. ... Aires: El Ateneo, 1929)

TABLE 6–18 PRICE OF CEREALS IN RELATION TO URBAN SALARIES (INDEX C/US)
(in gold pesos and in index numbers)
(base 1899:100)

Year	Cereal Prices[a] (in $ gold)	Urban Salaries (in $ gold)	C/US
1880	195	58	336
1881	175	60	291
1882	152	65	233
1883	123	73	168
1884	121	83	146
1885	89	69	129
1886	124	73	170
1887	104	83	125
1888	97	87	111
1889	100	100	100
1890	90	61	148
1891	124	47	263
1892	95	58	164
1893	89	68	131
1894	75	67	112
1895	71	75	95

[a] *Cereal prices represent a mean of the price of wheat and of corn.*

SOURCE: Material compiled by the author based on salary data from the archive of the Bagley Company and on cereal prices data from Cortés Conde, Halperin-Donghi, and de Torres, *Evolución del Comercio.*

this subject.[34] In order to arrive at a more accurate estimate, the price of grains has been deflated by the use of an index of salaries for industrial workers, and the new estimate is shown in Table 6–18.

During the entire first part of the 1890s, cereal prices, which had

[34] This also occurred with respect to salaries. See Juan Alvarez, *Las guerras civiles argentinas y el problema de Buenos Aires en la República Argentina* (Buenos Aires: Libreria y Editorial "La Facultad," Bernabe y cía, 1936). Nevertheless, another aspect is considered in the author's recent study; see Roberto Cortés Conde, "Evolución del salario urbano" (in preparation).

TABLE 6–19 PRICE OF CEREALS IN RELATION TO URBAN SALARIES, FORTNIGHTLY AVERAGE

1881–1884	234.80
1885–1889	127.00
1890–1894	163.60

fallen considerably in relation to salaries, achieved a significant recuperation, as Table 6–19 shows.

This situation is inverted after 1895, once more against the exporting sector, leading in 1899 to a monetary reform.

THE INSTITUTIONAL STRUCTURE

A condition and consequence of that same progress was the establishment of an institutional structure capable of assuring stability, peace, and security for capital investments, as well as a central government able to impose and enforce uniform legislation throughout the entire country and a justice system respected by all. That this structure be established by an authority known abroad was essential to the movement of capital and manpower.

INDICATORS OF GROWTH

In Table 6–20 some economic indicators are summarized which convey an idea of the growth process registered between 1880 and 1913 and also point to the differences of growth in various areas.

Some significant differences between Table 6–20 and Table 6–21 bear mention. Between 1880 and 1890 the category that shows the highest increase—312 percent—is the public debt, whereas imports rose 212 percent, the national income only 49 percent, and government expenses, 42 percent. From these figures the correlation between the public debt and imports may be deduced. If it is remembered that materials for the infrastructure comprised a large proportion of imports, the role of imports may be confirmed in analyzing the elements that make up the basic

TABLE 6–20 ECONOMIC INDICATORS BETWEEN 1880 AND 1890
(*in thousands of gold pesos and in index numbers*)
(*base 1880:100*)

		1880	1886	1890
Population	Thousands of Inhabitants	2.493	2.966	3.778
	IN	100	119	272
Cultivated Area	Thousands of Hectares	1.156	1.838	2.996
	IN	100[a]	159	260
Government Revenues	Thousands of Gold Pesos	19.594	30.396	29.144
	IN	100	155	149
Government Administrative Expenses	Thousands of Gold Pesos	26.919	39.179	38.146
	IN	100	146	142
Foreign Trade	Thousands of Gold Pesos	103.917	165.244	243.060
	IN	100	159	234
Exports	Thousands of Gold Pesos	58.381	69.835	100.819
	IN	100	120	173
Imports	Thousands of Gold Pesos	45.536	95.409	142.241
	IN	100	210	322
Total Public Debt	Thousands of Gold Pesos	86.313	117.154	355.762
	IN	100	136	412
Foreign Public Debt	Thousands of Gold Pesos	17.388	68.026	161.391
	IN	100	391	928

[a] *This figure is for 1878–1880.*

SOURCES: The author's elaboration based on statistics from E. Tornquist and Co., *The Economic Development;* República Argentina, *Extracto estadístico,* 1915; *Anuario de la Sociedad Rural Argentina* (Buenos Aires: 1928); República Argentina, *Resúmenes estadísticos retrospectivos* (1914); República Argentina, *Informes de la Dirección General de Estadística y Censos,* nos. 1–10; República Argentina, *Estadística* (1894, 1897, and 1902); *Argentine Year Book,* 1902, 1914, 1915–1916; República Argentina, *Memoria de Hacienda,* vol. 2 (1906); *Revista de Economía Argentina,* vol. 20, *Exposición sobre el estado económico y financiero de la República Argentina* (1893); J. Fred Rippy, *British Investments in Latin America 1822–1949* (Minneapolis, Minn.: University of Minnesota Press, 1959); John Williams, *Argentine International Trade.*

social capital. This is even clearer if the difference is observed between the categories of population and cultivated area and those of government revenues and administrative expenses, which in the early stage show less growth, even less than that of exports. Government expenses did not grow so markedly despite the in-

TABLE 6–21 ECONOMIC INDICATORS BETWEEN 1894 AND 1913
(in thousands of gold pesos and in index numbers)
(base 1894:100)

		1894	**1897**	**1902**	**1906**	**1913**
Population	Thousands of Inhabitants	3.857	4.234	4.872	5.524	7.482
	IN	100	110	126	143	194
Cultivated Area	Thousands of Hectares	4.457	5.372	9.115	13.898	24.091
	IN	100	120	204	312	540
Government Revenues	Thousands of Gold Pesos	34.178	51.441	65.404	100.751	153.692
	IN	100	150	191	295	445
Government Administrative Expenses	Thousands of Gold Pesos	40.114	61.010	85.335	118.911	177.513
	IN	100	152	213	296	442
Foreign Trade	Thousands of Gold Pesos	194.477	199.458	282.526	562.224	1015.383
	IN	100	102	145	290	522
Export	Thousands of Gold Pesos	101.688	101.169	179.487	292.254	519.156
	IN	100	99	176	288	510
Imports	Thousands of Gold Pesos	92.789	98.289	103.039	269.970	496.227
	IN	100	106	111	291	535
Total Public Debt	Thousands of Gold Pesos	393.396	438.283	435.655	379.560	544.722
	IN	100	111	111	96	138
Foreign Public Debts	Thousands of Gold Pesos	190.991	233.288	381.083	324.333	308.855
	IN	100	122	199	169	162
Foreign Capital	Thousands of Gold Pesos	837[a]	—	—	2.257[b]	3.250/
	IN	100	—	—	270	420

[a] *Estimate made by Minister of Finance Hansen in the* Memoria *presented to Congress in 1892.*
[b] *Data for 1910 and 1913 for V. Phelps,* International Economic Position of Argentina *(Philadelphia: University of Pennsylvania Press, 1938), p. 99, citing Schwenke's estimates from* Review of the River Plate.

SOURCES: See Table 6–20.

dignant criticism of many contemporaries: they grew in a lesser proportion than exports and population. The second period is different: exports mounted much more than imports and the public debt. The level of the national debt in absolute terms and in relation to exports diminished. One might say that the sequence of Argentine development began with a strong initial foreign indebtedness and was followed immediately by the incorporation of foreign capital. With some delay this all was reflected in the subsequent growth of exports, income, and government expenses.

Changes in Regional Structure and in Urbanization Patterns

One of the forms manifested by this pattern of development, which involved incorporation of lands for cultivation and the settlement of the Pampas, was the change of the regional structure and urbanization patterns. At the beginning of the nineteenth century the colonial axis leaned toward Potosí, the Upper Peruvian highway uniting Córdoba, Tucumán and Salta with present-day Bolivia was replaced by one along the river coast (Río de la Plata, Paraná, and Uruguay). During this third period the axis remained attached to a port, though one on the Atlantic rather than one on the river system. Thus, it penetrated deep into the center and south, forming the area known today as the Pampas.[35]

The shift in regional axis was reflected in the appearance of a new urban pattern. This was no longer the old Spanish colonial outpost or the river port center, but the rural village which arose with its railroad station as the most characteristic phenomenon of the new agricultural Argentina. The significance of the new settlements in the interior zones and the relative loss of old coastal zones can best be perceived in the province of Buenos Aires.

There is no doubt that this new regional axis generated a strong concentration of wealth in the zone it covered, a concentration that was stimulated by the presence of new activities to satisfy a market

[35] See Roberto Cortés Conde, "Tendencias en el crecimiento de la población urbana en Argentina," *Actas del 38 Congreso de Americanistas* (Stuttgart, Germany, 1968).

TABLE 6–22 GROWTH OF VILLAGES
(*in quantity and index numbers*)
(*base 1869:100*)

	1869		**1881**		**1895**		**1914**	
	N	*IN*	*N*	*IN*	*N*	*IN*	*N*	*IN*
Northern Zone[a]	6	100	8	133	16	266	23	383
Central Zone[a]	5	100	7	140	25	500	42	820

[a] *The northern zone constitutes the coastal zone, the central zone is the new interior zone.*

SOURCE: Roberto Cortés Conde and Nancy L. de Nisnovich, "El Dessarrollo Agrícola en el Proceso de Urbanización," Schaedel et al., *Urbanización y proceso social en America* (Lima: Instituto de Estudios Peruanos, 1972).

which was reached once transportation costs had been lowered by the growth of railroads. Though here, too, an existing advantage generated numerous others that perpetuated and increased it, in Argentina one fact must be borne in mind, which, though quite evident, is apparently often forgotten: the pampas area, for climatic and ecological reasons, possesses the land that is most suitable for cultivation. Unlike the United States, the best lands were not far from the coasts.

THE EFFECT OF GROWTH ON THE DOMESTIC SECTOR: INDUSTRIES

One of the sometimes neglected aspects of this period is that expansion was not restricted merely to the external sector. For a series of reasons such as the rise in population, which in Argentina was translated into a rise in national income,[36] and the establishment of a transportation network, there emerged a national market, a market previously fragmented in great measure not only by provincial barriers and customs laws, but also by enormous transportation costs. The presence of that market determined the appearance of industries destined to supply it, and the presence of

[36] This is because the reduced market in Argentina stemmed from lack of population, rather than from a large population with a very low income, as in other areas.

TABLE 6–23 PERSONNEL EMPLOYED IN INDUSTRIES IN 1895 AND 1914

Years	**Personnel**
1895	175,682
1914	410,201

SOURCE: Argentina, *Segundo Censo Nacional,* 1895; República Argentina. *Tercer Censo Nacional,* 1914 (Buenos Aires, Talleres Gráficos de L. J. Rosco y Cía, 1916).

TABLE 6–24 CAPITAL OF INDUSTRIAL ESTABLISHMENTS IN 1895 AND 1914 (*in millions of pesos*)

Years	**Capital in National Pesos**
1895	327,397,366
1914	1,787,662,295

SOURCE: Argentina, *Segundo Censo Nacional,* 1895; Argentina, *Tercer Censo Nacional,* 1914.

raw materials close to the places of manufacture led to the emergence of other industries geared to input sources. In some instances, such as food articles, the two prerequisites were united. In others, for example, meat packing plants, the market was to some degree foreign. Still others had the disadvantage of requiring a large proportion of imported inputs, a disadvantage which Argentine industry would have for a long time. Between 1895 and 1914 Argentine industries evolved in the manner shown in Tables 6–23 and 6–24.

The fact that capital increased more than personnel does not signify a tendency toward concentration in Argentine industry at that time. What it does mean, however, is the appearance of an industrial manufacturing phase as a consequence of the disappear-

TABLE 6–25 COMPOSITION OF ARGENTINE IMPORTS IN 1896 AND 1914
(*in percentages*)

Years	Foodstuffs	Beverages	Textiles and Clothes	Raw Materials and Manufactures	Total
1896	16.0	8.0	34.0	42.0	100
1914	9.5	3.0	20.5	67.10	100

SOURCE: *Anuario de la Dirección General de Estadística correspondiente a 1896* (Buenos Aires, 1897). *Anuario de la Dirección General de Estadística correspondiente a 1914* (Buenos Aires, 1915).

ance of numerous artisan workshops with limited capital and the appearance of a more capital-intensive industrial spectrum.

COMPOSITION OF INDUSTRY

That industries were devoted principally to the manufacture of domestic raw materials (in other words, they were industries derived from agriculture and cattle) and that when not directed toward the foreign sector, they were geared to supplying the most immediate domestic consumption is not surprising. A more precise view of the modification of the industrial structure can be obtained indirectly by studying in what manner imports were substituted. Table 6–25 reveals the decrease in imports in consumer goods categories (food, beverages, and even textiles), while raw materials and industrial goods increased.

LOCATION

The location of industries was determined by various factors:

1. For those which used imported raw materials (or energy) by nearness to ports.

2. For those which processed domestic raw materials: (a) if they were destined for the domestic market, by where these re-

TABLE 6–26 INDUSTRIAL ESTABLISHMENTS PER PROVINCE IN 1895 AND 1914

	1895	1914
Capital	8,439	9,947
Province of Buenos Aires	5,576	14,560
Santa Fe	2,678	4,042
Mendoza	—	1,794
Córdoba	—	1,369
Entre Ríos	—	1,305
Salta	—	1,704
Catamarca	—	431

SOURCE: Argentina, *Segundo Censo Nacional,* 1895; Argentina, *Tercer Censo Nacional,* 1914.

sources were found; (b) if they were destined for the external market, by where the ports of exportation were located.

There is no doubt that the railroad network was an important factor in reducing transference costs for industries using both domestic and imported raw materials. That this pattern evolved as it did and not otherwise is due not only to the investors' interest in the foreign market over the domestic, but more directly because the main Argentine agrarian area corresponded to the area of foreign interest.

ARGENTINA AT THE EVE OF WORLD WAR I

By the eve of World War I Argentina had gone through an important process; in fifty years its growth had been extraordinary. From being a poor backward country it had emerged with one of the highest product per capita levels in the world.[37] But it went

[37] Mulhall, *Handbook of the River Plate,* shows the product per capita of Argentina in relation to other countries in pounds sterling:

Argentina	130
Australia	343
Canada	196
Great Britain	247
France	224
United States	210

beyond that. The entire country had changed, not only the rural landscape where the desert had given way to seas of wheat and trees and dwellings, revealing the presence of humans in a formerly empty landscape, but the cities where poor, austere structures—including the dwellings of the wealthiest—were replaced by a style which mirrored the new wealth and strove to repeat the style of the great European metropolises. Traces still remain of those times which marked Buenos Aires as one of the great cities of the world. But it went even beyond that: the population changed. From almost demographic stagnation (or, at least, extremely limited growth), it shifted to powerful expansion. This expansion, a result of the massive incorporation of foreigners, within a few decades effected a substantial change in the composition of the population. As for the level of the economy, the structure of production and exports was diversified. From a set of only two elements, hides and wool, it became a much more diversified spectrum with the addition of grains (chiefly corn, wheat, and flax) and, later, meat production. The country possessed a transportation network previously lacking and a population scattered over a large portion of its territory, of which the richest portion had been formerly uninhabited.

The process of industrial development was hindered initially by a limitation which has not been given enough attention: the lack of manpower that persisted until almost the end of the century. Despite this lack, at least until 1890 the major public works competed with the rural sector for available manpower. More than the crisis of 1890, monetary measures which signified the raising of prices on imported products acted as an undeclared protective barrier in promoting the development of industries that, though in no way comparable to those of more advanced countries, were respectable nevertheless. In any event, the Argentine industry that did not manufacture agricultural or cattle products from the onset had to import its supply of raw materials.[38]

The growth of population and income, plus the establishment of a transportation network covering most of the country, meant the formation of a market on a national scale. The domestic sector not

38 See Lucio Geller, "El crecimiento industrial argentino hasta 1914 y la teoría del bien primario exportable," in *El Trimestre Económico,* vol. 37, no. 148 (October–December 1970).

only demanded manufactured products (food and textiles, first), but it also competed with the foreign sector for the supply of exportable products.[39] Although labor's share in the national income rose in relation to other sectors, due basically to a notable rise in occupation, this does not mean that labor in per capita terms has been the most favored sector. Data obtained in other studies[40] reveal that from the second five-year period of the twentieth century the landholding sector derived a much greater income than the other sectors of society. Landholders maintained a virtual monopoly, not by virtue of property control itself, but because most of the fertile lands were already being cultivated at the same time that demand for them continued (around 1914).

To conclude delineation of this rapid survey, it may be observed that at that time two circumstances were also evident:

1. Given the limited availability of fertile lands, the rate of growth, if subordinated to the extent of crops (including artificial cattle feed), was already declining and was later to decline drastically.

2. The rise in domestic demand assumed increasing competition for exportable production.

These circumstances, prior to and independent of the effects produced on foreign demand by the crisis of 1929, had their effect on the problems manifest in Argentina after the *belle époque.*

39 The percentage of exports in the country's production varied in the following manner:

1900–1904	54 percent
1940–1944	22 percent
1950–1954	22 percent

See United Nations, *Análisis y proyecciones del desarrollo económico de la Argentina* (Mexico City, 1959), p. 23.

40 See Roberto Cortés Conde, *Evolución de los precios de cereales, renta y salarios* (in preparation).

7
CONCLUSION

In the preceding pages, the author wished to sketch some of the features of the evolution of the economies of these countries between the second half of the nineteenth century and 1930 that share as a common characteristic an expansion linked to the growth of exports of primary products. It was observed that the factors which stimulated their growth as well as those that determined their later evolution were conditioned in great measure by the specific circumstances in each country or region: its conditions, resources, geographical location, climate, the composition of its population, and its degree of social and political development.[1]

Although there was a factor external to all of these countries, the existence of the demand for primary products in the most advanced countries and a degree of technological evolution which permitted the reduction of transportation costs and, therefore, the possibility of bringing markets closer, this does not seem enough to explain their different evolution and the complexity of their development. Facts such as the existence of a resource that might be exhaustible—guano in Peru—or that would not be exhausted—agriculture with a crop that is renewed annually—might be more important than was assumed in relation to the effect that an export activity might have on the economy's future development. The different proportions in which labor was used in extensive cattle raising in plantation agriculture or in family agriculture would

[1] The nature of the region's resources and the initial conditions in which the exploitation of the primary good occurs, determine to a great extent, according to Baldwin, the technological nature (production functions) and its effects on the development of the whole economy. Cf. Robert E. Baldwin, "Patterns of Development in Newly Settled Regions," in John Friedman and William Alonso, eds., *Regional Development and Planning* (Cambridge, Mass.: The M.I.T. Press, 1964).

have diverse consequences on the distribution of income.[2] Therefore, it would also have diverse consequences on the formation of an internal market and on its effects in the growth that the external sector would produce on the economy as a whole.

For example, the growth of exports due to extensive cattle raising in the Río de la Plata before 1850 had different effects on the domestic sector from those due to the production of hides after 1890. Also, in spite of having features that are similar to other economies with an export base, the production of sugar in a plantation economy had very different effects on the whole, since it is more capital-intensive and pays very low monetary salaries or nothing at all, if it is based on the exploitation of slave labor. In other cases, for different reasons (monoproduction, lack of internal demand,[3] and so forth) the initial situation in which the only outlet for exportable products was the external market[4] continues to be the rule. In still other instances, on the other hand, the domestic sector began to compete with the external one in the production of exportable products as in Argentina. This did not necessarily assume the end of dependence on the external sector, but rather a new situation that, although demonstrating a level of greater development, was perhaps more difficult and complex than the previous one.

The different nature of the inputs, those that are supplied from abroad or internally for each type of production, also had diverse effects (linkages) on the development of domestic or resident industries.[5] Although in some cases these effects were almost

[2] Douglas North, "Agriculture in Regional Economic Growth," *Journal of Farm Economics,* vol. 61, no. 5 (December 1959), pp. 949–950. About this, see chap. 1, n. 14, above.

[3] The lack of internal demand may result from low incomes, a lack of population (for consumer goods) or because industries that might use certain raw materials do not exist.

[4] This is the assumption implicit in the theory of "Vent for surplus." Cf. chap. 1, above, H. Myint, "The Classical Theory of International Trade and the Underdeveloped Countries," *The Economic Journal* 68 (1958): 321 and Richard E. Caves, " 'Vent for Surplus' Models of Trade and Growth," in Robert Baldwin et al., *Trade, Growth and the Balance of Payments* (Chicago: Rand McNally and Co., 1965).

[5] The concept of linkage was developed by A. Hirschman, *The Strategy of Economic Development* (New Haven, Conn.: Yale University Press, 1965), p. 100.

imperceptible (guano would be an extreme instance), in others, such as Mexico and Argentina, they were quite important. The existence of a political power with more or less control over this process should also be taken into account although in general the specific analysis of each case is not developed. In Chile the external sector redistributed some part of its income to the domestic sector through increasing taxes and through a complex exchange mechanism that was utilized after 1930.

From the analysis of each of the cases considered, the conclusion is reached that a version that limits the study of the evolution of these countries' economies to the fluctuations of external demand and the flows of capital and of labor is at least simplified. Although no one doubts the importance and the role of external factors, it is necessary to bear in mind the specific characteristics in the development of each concrete case, in which many other internal factors are invariably at play. If not, one loses much of the richness and complexity of the process with its advances and retrogressions. Here it may be deduced that it seems oversimplified to affirm that once the external factors disappear, the development engendered by them is halted and that these countries return to their previous condition of backwardness. Although the fact that the growth of exports alone did not signify in all cases the overcoming of their underdeveloped condition and this "external oriented growth" has left problems that are not easy to resolve, the fact that in many cases this growth resulted in more enduring contributions cannot be ignored. An important transportation network, basic public works, and, although not always, an internal market are some of its legacies. Certainly serious problems appear in its evolution: violent fluctuations of income and the necessity of adjusting to changing technological and market conditions, among others.[6] In order to understand their

[6] The primary goods-producing countries also were liable to problems derived from unfavorable terms of exchange. Prebisch, Singer and Nurkse dealt with them and maintained to some degree the need to further industrialization for the domestic market as a means to overcome these problems. Cf. United Nations, *Economic Survey of Latin America, 1949,* Secretariat of the Economic Commission for Latin America (Raúl Prebisch) New York, 1951, pp. 46–47; H. W. Singer, "U.S. Foreign Investment in Underdeveloped Areas: The Distribution of Zones between Investing and Borrowing Countries," *The American Economic Review,* vol. 40, no. 2 (May 1950), p. 473;

evolutions, it is necessary to consider their characteristics in detail, that is, each of the factors that participate in a process that has been described many times but is not thoroughly known. This is to a certain extent what we have tried to outline in the previous chapter. Furthermore it should be pointed out, perhaps, that these societies do not necessarily have to pass through predetermined stages. Also, that certain economies are considered more or less successful depends in large measure on the standard by which they are defined as such. To achieve this it would be better to try to avoid a frame of reference that, although implicit, is almost always present: that is, to assume that these countries ought to follow the patterns of development of those which were the earliest to develop.[7] Finally, we should discard once and for all the rather weakly founded notion of deviated development, which assumes a compulsory pattern that for some obscure reason has to be followed.

---

and Ragnar Nurske, *Problemas de Formación de Capital* (Mexico City: Fondo de Cultura Económica, 1960), p. 31.

7 In this sense what Harold A. Innis points out is very important, in *Essays in Canadian Economic History* (Toronto, Canada: University of Toronto Press, 1965), p. 3.

A new country presents certain definite problems which appear to be more or less insoluble from the standpoint of the application of economic theory as worked out in the older highly industrialized countries. Economic history consequently becomes more important as a tool by which the economic theory of the old countries can be amended.

INDEX

74 75 76 77 78 79 80 12 11 10 9 8 7 6 5 4 3 2 1